240 Family Devotions From Psalms & Proverbs

# NOT-
# So-Quiet Times 2

## Tracy Harrast

Standard
Publishing
Cincinnati, Ohio

Standard Publishing, a division of Standex International Corporation, Cincinnati, Ohio.
© 2000 by Tracy L. Harrast. All rights reserved.
Bean Sprouts™ and the Bean Sprouts design logo are
trademarks of Standard Publishing.

Scripture taken from the HOLY BIBLE, NEW INTERNATIONAL VERSION®. NIV®.
Copyright © 1973, 1978, 1984 by International Bible Society. Used by
permission of Zondervan Publishing House. All rights reserved.

Printed in the United States of America.
ISBN 0-7847-1090-2

Project editor: Laura Derico. Design: Liz Howe Design.
Typesetting by Andrew Quach. Author photo by Deborah Safaie.

07  06  05  04  03  02  01  00        5  4  3  2  1

The Library of Congress has catalogued the first volume of this work as follows:
Harrast, Tracy L.
Not-so-quiet times: 240 family devotions based on the words of Jesus / by Tracy L. Harrast.
p. cm.
ISBN 0-7847-1041-4
1. Children–Prayer-books and devotions–English. 2. Family–Prayer-books and devotions–English.
I. Title.

BV4571.2.H375 2000
249–dc21                                                        99-055975

## Dedication

To Glenda McCloskey, whose soul is filled with light. Your relationship with Jesus inspires me, your insights teach me, and your compassion touches me. You are a Proverbs 17:17 friend who loves at all times.

# WHAT'S INSIDE
## This Book

## More Good Stuff

# GETTING STARTED
## and Sticking With It!

## A Few Pointers

⊙ **Find the time of day that works best for your family devotions.** First thing in the morning? Before breakfast? With after-school snacks? During dinner? Before your kids' favorite show? After baths? Before bedtime?

⊙ **If you miss your regular time, grab a minute when you can.** Skim the devotion yourself and then talk about it on the go. You can even discuss the day's verse with the kids while you're reaching for the baby shampoo or waiting for a red light to change—but don't drop the book in the tub or out the car window!

Find the Time

⊙ **Involve the whole family!** If both parents can be involved in the devotions and take turns teaching them, the kids understand that God's Word is important to both their mom and their dad. Besides, devotions are more fun if the whole family is involved!

## Stay Flexible!

✸ **Don't hesitate to customize the devotions** for your family. If your youngest kids can't write, let them draw or dictate to you while the others write. If any memory verses are too long for the youngest kids, select a shorter section of the verse for them to memorize. Feel free to use other translations of the Bible if you wish.

✸ **Don't be discouraged** if the kids are rambunctious at first while testing their boundaries. Keep things casual (translate: no assigned seats in the family room) so the kids don't tune you out because things are too stiff. The less the devotion feels like school, the more they'll like it. Remember, "Do not exasperate your children; instead, bring them up in the training and instruction of the Lord" (Ephesians 6:4).

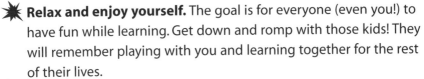 **Relax and enjoy yourself.** The goal is for everyone (even you!) to have fun while learning. Get down and romp with those kids! They will remember playing with you and learning together for the rest of their lives.

**Each day before you skim the devotion,** ask the Lord to give the kids listening ears and to plant his Word deep into everyone's heart. Then let the Holy Spirit lead the way. If he gives you a different way to teach the devotion, go for it!

**When you're tempted to skip devotion time,** repeat to yourself over and over: "It's important! It's quick! It's easy!"

**Usually if you just give the devotions a quick skim,** you're good to go. If you can, glance at a week's worth at a time. (Sunday afternoon might be a good time.) If the Attention Grabbers use any materials at all, the items will usually be things you already have on hand, but glance at the supply list on pages 257-260 to be sure you will have everything you need. On days when you don't have time or materials, just skip the Attention Grabber and go on to the Living It section.

# Keep With It

... **Even if** you only have time to read the day's verse.

... **Even if** you're on vacation.

... **Even if** somebody has the chicken pox.

... **Even if** you've missed a day or a week.

**Don't let anything stop you from doing devotions.**

*Fix these words of mine in your hearts and minds.... Teach them to your children, talking about them when you sit at home and when you walk along the road, when you lie down and when you get up.*
*Deuteronomy 11:18, 19*

# HOW TO LEAD
## These Devotions

## Memory Verse

You will be amazed at how much faster kids memorize than adults. Hide God's Word in their hearts and they'll use the verses throughout their lives.

◎ Provide a Know-It-By-Heart Chart for each family member (page 261). Photocopy the chart if you need more than two.

◎ Try to memorize a verse each day or as often as possible.

◎ See tips for memorization on pages 14–15.

## Attention Grabber

The fun you'll have during these activities will unite your family, help the kids focus, and make the devotions memorable.

◎ When an activity requires extra time or slightly unusual materials, you will find a simple option, too. If you have the time and materials, do the longer version. If time or supplies are limited, do the faster version.

◎ If you're in a pinch, don't worry if you need to skip over this section and get right to Living It. Never let lack of time for this section keep you from doing the devotion.

◎ If you can, skim these briefly in advance. Check the supplies list on pages 257–260 weekly or monthly to be sure you have everything you'll need. You will probably already have most of the items on hand. Some activities require only imagination!

◎ In most cases, pique their curiosity with the Attention Grabber before reading the Memory Verse. But if your time is too limited, let the older kids do the Attention Grabbers as fun follow-ups.

# Living It

This is when you make the point. Explain the verse and show the kids how to apply it to their lives.

- ◉ You may wish to begin by reading the Bible passage cited at the top of the devotion. If you read all the passages, by the end of this book you will have read all of Psalms and Proverbs. However, not all the verses in a passage may apply to the particular lesson. Skim the passage first and choose which verses you want to read.
- ◉ This section is written so you can read it out of the book; but it will be more interesting to the kids if you use your own words.
- ◉ Add examples from family members' lives whenever possible.

# Discussion Questions

This section gets the kids flexing their brain muscles.

- ◉ Some of the questions are rhetorical. Let the kids know which they need to just think about and which they should answer aloud.
- ◉ Pay attention to the kids' responses to see what kind of follow-up, one-on-one discussion they may need.
- ◉ Some questions are geared toward older kids. It's OK to skip these with younger children.

# Prayer Prompter

Always end the devotion with prayer so the kids will learn to rely on God. Praying together will draw your family close.

- ◉ Let the Prayer Prompter focus your family's attention on the spiritual lesson God is impressing on your hearts.
- ◉ Each day ask everyone in the family to share at least one prayer request or praise. In addition to praying for God's help to apply the devotion, pray for everyone's personal needs.

# TIPS
## for Memorizing Bible Verses

- When memorizing verses, memorize the references, too.

- Recite the day's verse several times while preparing and eating breakfast. Ask each child to repeat it at least once before leaving for school or beginning homeschool studies.

- Write the verse on the bathroom mirror with a dry-erase marker stored in the bathroom drawer.

- If there's enough time, you or the kids can write the verse on their lunch sacks or paper napkins.

- Buy small dot stickers in a different color for each family member. Whoever remembers the day's verse at dinnertime gets to stick his or her color of dot on a Know-It-By-Heart Chart (page 261).

- At dinnertime, ask who thought of the verse during the day. How did it help?

- Offer special incentives to be awarded on Fridays (for example, a video rental or trip to the park) if everyone in the family can remember all five of the week's memory verses.

- Music makes verses easier to memorize. Consider buying cassettes that teach Bible verses through songs. Or simply make up your own songs by singing each verse to a familiar tune (such as "Mary Had a Little Lamb").

- Use the day's verse as a password that everyone must recite to enter the house or one another's bedrooms.

- Tape verses to the TV remote control and computer monitor.

- Seal the verses between sticky sides of two pieces of Con-Tact self-adhesive cover. Cut into shapes. Wet these "water stickers," and they'll stick to the bathtub or shower wall for memorizing while you scrub-a-dub-dub.

- Tape copies of verses to food or treats the kids can have once they memorize the verse. Try wrapping a verse around the shell of a hard-boiled egg or a stick of gum.

- Tape the verses to the back of the cereal box so kids will stare at them while they eat.

- Have the kids tape the day's verse around their pencils so they can read it during breaks at school.

- Let the kids write verses on the sidewalk with colored chalk.

- Set monthly goals for the family together. Have everyone help those who are struggling until they meet the goal so you can have a family Memorization Celebration.

# Like a Tree by Water

## Memory Verse

*He is like a tree planted by streams of water, which yields its fruit in season and whose leaf does not wither. Whatever he does prospers (Psalm 1:3).*

## Attention Grabber

Place a stalk of celery in a jar of water containing five drops of red or blue food coloring. Point out that eventually the leaves will be colored red or blue because the celery absorbs the colored water. Explain that a tree's roots absorb water the same way. If you do not have celery, cut a clipping from a houseplant for each child and place the clippings in jars of clear water. Tell the kids that eventually the clippings will grow roots to absorb water the way a tree's roots can absorb water from a stream.

## Living It

A tree planted near a stream has the strong roots and water it needs to be able to grow fruit. If we have a close relationship with the Lord in which we obey him and study his Word, we are like that tree. We are "rooted and established in love" (Ephesians 3:17) and Jesus gives us living water (John 4:10-14). Living water is the Holy Spirit (John 7:38, 39). When we let the Holy Spirit work in us, he grows fruit in our lives: love, joy, peace, patience, kindness, goodness, faithfulness, gentleness, and self-control (Galatians 5:22, 23).

## Discussion Questions

- What are your needs? How can God meet them through his Holy Spirit?
- How does feeling God's love make you more loving to others?
- How does obeying God meet your needs?

## Prayer Prompter

Thank you for providing for us through your Holy Spirit. Please produce the fruit of the Spirit in us.

# God Is My Shield
## Psalms 2, 3

### Memory Verse
*But you are a shield around me, O Lord; you bestow glory on me and lift up my head (Psalm 3:3).*

### Attention Grabber
Let each family member make a paper plate into a shield by attaching a handle made out of duct tape to the back of the plate. Let each person draw Christian symbols (a cross, a dove, a Bible, a fish, etc.) on her shield. Then have everyone crumple sheets of scrap paper into wads. Have a paper wad war in which everyone fends off the wads with the shields.

### Living It
No matter what your situation, you can trust God and feel protected knowing he is in control of all things. Sometimes you may feel discouraged. When a person is discouraged, she might hang her head down and look sad. If you feel like hanging your head down, run to God. Take time to read his Word and pray. He will show you how much he loves you and how great he thinks you are. He will "lift your head."

### Discussion Questions
◉ What are ways that God has protected you?
◉ When you have been discouraged, how has God "lifted your head"?

### Prayer Prompter
Thank you for protecting us. Thank you for reassuring and encouraging us when we come to you.

7/21/08

# Angry? Don't Sin
## Psalm 4:1-4

## Memory Verse
*In your anger do not sin; when you are on your beds, search your hearts and be silent (Psalm 4:4).*

## Attention Grabber
Pace and clench your teeth as if you are angry. Then count to ten to pretend to calm yourself. After you get to ten, act perfectly normal and ask, "Why do people suggest counting to ten when you're angry?" Let everyone have a chance to answer.

## Living It
If we don't calm ourselves when we feel angry, it is easy to say or do something wrong. If we yell at people or put them down, we damage our relationships with them. Our words can make them feel bad about themselves and us. First Corinthians 13:5 says that love is "not easily angered, it keeps no record of wrongs." Almost every act of violence that is shown on the news could have been prevented if the people involved had learned to control their tempers. What are healthy ways to release anger? (pray, exercise, clean, write your feelings on paper, etc.)

## Discussion Questions
- Why does God want you to be quiet and search your heart? What does he want you to search for in your heart?
- Instead of getting mad, what are some better ways to handle conflicts with people?

## Prayer Prompter
Please help us learn to release our anger in healthy ways without sinning.

# Sleep Peacefully
## Psalm 4:5-8

### Memory Verse

*I will lie down and sleep in peace, for you alone, O Lord, make me dwell in safety (Psalm 4:8).*

### Attention Grabber

Ask the kids to sing lullabies they remember from when they were little. Ask if they have ever counted sheep to try to get to sleep.

### Living It

Sometimes it is hard to sleep if we are worried or afraid. At times like that, it is good to remember the memory verse from Psalm 4:8. We can sleep knowing that God is always awake and watching over us (Psalm 121:2, 3).

### Discussion Questions

◉ What nightmares have you had? What specific truths about God could help calm your fears? (For example, knowing God is more powerful than anything can help you not be afraid of the monsters you dream about.)

◉ When you feel restless and can't get to sleep, what do you do? How can prayer help you sleep in peace?

### Prayer Prompter

When we have restless nights, please help us to trust you to watch over us. Please give us peace so we can sleep well.

Sleep Peacefully

# Living With God

## Memory Verse

*You are not a God who takes pleasure in evil; with you the wicked cannot dwell (Psalm 5:4).*

## Attention Grabber

Have the kids imagine that they are old enough to have apartments and that they need roommates. Have each of them make up a classified ad for the ideal roommate. Point out that they wouldn't want to live with a person who wanted to do bad things all the time. Emphasize that only the righteous can live with God.

## Living It

Everyone has done bad things. Everyone has sinned, including you and me (Romans 3:23; 1 John 1:10). Sinners can't live with God. God is just. "He will punish those who do not know God and do not obey the gospel of our Lord Jesus" and they will be "shut out from the presence of the Lord" (2 Thessalonians 1:8, 9). We all need Jesus as our personal Savior! The only way we can have our sins removed and be able to live in God's presence is to trust Jesus (John 14:6). We are made righteous (right with God) through believing in Jesus (Romans 10:4). (If your child seems ready to trust Jesus, see page 270 for help.)

## Discussion Questions

◉ Since the wicked can't dwell with God, should you avoid God when you sin? Why or why not? (No! He wants us to come to him and repent.)

◉ How can you live with God?

## Prayer Prompter

We want to live with you forever. Thank you for loving us enough to send your Son to be the way for us to live with you.

# How Majestic!
## Psalms 7:1–8:2

### Memory Verse
*O Lord, our Lord, how majestic is your name in all the earth! You have set your glory above the heavens (Psalm 8:1).*

### Attention Grabber
Sing the worship song based on this psalm, if you know it. Or have your family describe God with words that begin with each letter of the alphabet. (For example, "God is awesome. God blesses. God cares.") Feel free to skip difficult letters or to use words like "eXcellent."

### Living It
When approaching a king or queen, people bow and say "Your Majesty." To say the Lord's name is majestic means his name is kingly and grand. God's name is more than just a word. His name represents who he is. God is king of everything in the universe. He is glorious, and so are the great things he has done. One of the Ten Commandments is, "You shall not misuse the name of the Lord your God" (Exodus 20:7). Misusing God's name shows disrespect for who he is.

### Discussion Questions
- What have you seen in nature that made you feel awed by God's creative power?
- Sometimes when people worship God's majesty, their eyes fill with tears that aren't caused by sadness. What do you think they are feeling? Have you ever felt that way?

### Prayer Prompter
We are in awe of you, God. Please help us to treat your name with respect always.

# When I Consider
## Psalm 8:3-9

### Memory Verse
*When I consider your heavens, the work of your fingers, the moon and the stars, which you have set in place, what is man that you are mindful of him, the son of man that you care for him? (Psalm 8:3, 4).*

### Attention Grabber
Go outside together after dark and look at the moon and stars. Show the kids how to find the Big Dipper and other constellations. If it's daytime, make star stampers by cutting apples in half crosswise. Dip the apple halves in tempera paint and press them on paper to see the star pattern in the center of each print.

### Living It
Looking up into the gigantic sky can make us feel very small. It's amazing to think that as tiny as we are compared to the huge universe, God still cares about each of us. He even cares for creatures that are smaller than us! Jesus said that since God feeds the birds, we can trust him to take care of us because God considers us more valuable than birds (Matthew 6:26).

### Discussion Questions
◉ How do you feel when you look at the stars?
◉ How can you tell that you are important to God?

### Prayer Prompter
Thank you for caring about each of us, Lord.

# Tell His Wonders
## Psalm 9:1-6

### Memory Verse
*I will praise you, O Lord, with all my heart; I will tell of all your wonders (Psalm 9:1).*

### Attention Grabber
Sing the praise song based on this psalm, if you know it. Give each child black paper and colored chalk (or white paper and markers) to draw a picture representing something God has done in his life. Have each person tell about his picture.

### Living It
When have you been so excited about something that you could hardly stop talking about it? As we get to know God and see him do great works in our lives, we want to tell others. As we grow closer to him, we become more confident and secure. We don't worry as much about what other people think. Also, he helps us to love others more, which makes us want to tell them about him. When we tell others about the wonderful things God has done in our lives, it encourages them to have more faith.

### Discussion Questions
◉ Why is it encouraging to hear people praise God by telling what he has done in their lives?
◉ What has God done in your life that might be encouraging for others to hear?

### Prayer Prompter
We praise you for all you have done in our lives, Lord. Please help us to know you better and to see your work in our lives more. Give us the courage to praise you to others, too.

# God Is My Refuge
## Psalm 9:7-20

## Memory Verse

*The Lord is a refuge for the oppressed, a stronghold in times of trouble (Psalm 9:9).*

## Attention Grabber

If you have time, take a walk with your family in a nearby park, or simply step outside into your backyard. Explain that a refuge is a safe place. Ask the kids where various types of animals take refuge from storms and predators.

## Living It

In some games, "home" is the one place where a person is safe. In life, God is our "home." We can tell him our problems without worrying that he'll gossip about them. We can ask him for advice, and he'll guide us to make the right decision. We can ask him to do something for us, and he won't let us down. He can be our trustworthy source of strength and safety when we have trouble in our lives.

## Discussion Questions

◉ When you have problems, how is God's love your refuge?
◉ How can God's truth keep you safe? How can his truth make you strong?

## Prayer Prompter

Thank you for being our protection and strength. Help us to remember to stay with you in times of trouble.

# Room for God

7/22/05

**Psalm 10**

## Memory Verse

*In his pride the wicked does not seek him; in all his thoughts there is no room for God (Psalm 10:4).*

## Attention Grabber

Beforehand, photocopy "My Week" from page 264 for each family member. Or let each person write a similar schedule. Help the kids plan times during the week when they will read the Bible and pray.

## Living It

What does the word "seek" mean? (to look for something) Some people don't look for God because they are so prideful that they think they do not need him. They spend little time, if any, thinking about God. They keep their minds and lives so full of other things that they don't have time for the Lord. It's important to have a close relationship with God and to keep our thoughts on him. A simple way to help ourselves do this is to schedule times during the week for Bible study and prayer.

## Discussion Questions

- What things might keep you from praying and reading the Bible this week? How can you avoid these things?
- What in your life encourages you to seek God and think about him?

## Prayer Prompter

Thank you for wanting to be in our lives. Please remind us to seek you and to think about you often.

# God's Flawless Words
## Psalms 11, 12

### Memory Verse

*The words of the Lord are flawless, like silver refined in a furnace of clay, purified seven times (Psalm 12:6).*

### Attention Grabber

Show the kids a piece of silver jewelry or another silver item. If you have silver dinnerware, let each child polish a piece. Emphasize that silver goes though a process called refining in which impurities are removed from it. This leaves the silver pure and flawless.

### Living It

God's words are completely true. You can trust them. Like refined silver, his words don't have any flaws. Like precious metal, they are valuable.

### Discussion Questions

- Have you ever relied on a promise from God? What was the promise? How did God keep his promise to you?
- Why is God's Word valuable to you?

### Prayer Prompter

We trust you, Lord. Thank you for always being truthful and faithful. Help us to learn what is in your written Word, the Bible.

# Trust His Love
**Psalm 13**

## Memory Verse

*But I trust in your unfailing love; my heart rejoices in your salvation (Psalm 13:5).*

## Attention Grabber

Show the kids an alarm clock. Explain that you trust this clock to wake you in the morning because it doesn't fail. A reliable clock is one that doesn't start and stop, but instead runs consistently.

## Living It

God's love is reliable. It is consistent. It doesn't start and then stop and then start again. God loves us all of the time, no matter what. Because his love is unfailing, we can trust him. We don't have to worry that anything we do or say will change his love for us. Every time we go to him in prayer, he is happy to hear from us. If we believe in Jesus and follow him, we can rejoice that we will live forever in heaven with God, who loves us so much.

## Discussion Questions

- Do you think God loves you more than your parents do? Why or why not?
- How does knowing you are loved by God help you?

## Prayer Prompter

Thank you for loving us all of the time. Thank you for sending your Son to provide the way for us to live forever with you.

# God Is Real

## Memory Verse

*The fool says in his heart, "There is no God" (Psalm 14:1).*

## Attention Grabber

Beforehand, secretly tell a family member to completely ignore you when you talk to her. While everyone gathers for the devotion, say several things to this person until the others ask why she is acting like you don't exist. Ask, "How do you think God feels when some people pretend he isn't there?"

## Living It

The fool in Psalm 14 is an unwise person. He is a person who does evil things and has turned away from God. He is a person who denies that God exists. Many people believe in God, but many don't. Some don't believe God is real because they don't want to admit they sin and need to repent (Romans 1:18). But "what may be known about God is plain to them" (Romans 1:19). Proof of God's existence is all around us. We're surrounded by God's creations. Romans 1:20 says people don't have an excuse not to believe in God because they can see God's power and divine nature by looking at all he has made. When we seek God, we can have more understanding and learn to make wise choices.

## Discussion Questions

- What is some evidence you've seen that makes you believe in God?
- How will your day today be different from the day of someone who doesn't believe in God?

## Prayer Prompter

We believe in you! Thank you for showing us that you are real. Help us always to seek you and your wisdom.

# God Counsels
## Psalms 16, 17

### Memory Verse
*I will praise the Lord, who counsels me; even at night my heart instructs me (Psalm 16:7).*

### Attention Grabber
Let the kids listen to your heartbeat and beat the rhythm on a tabletop. Ask, "Is this what people mean when they say to listen to your heart?" (No, they mean to listen to what you know deep down inside is the truth.)

### Living It
Sometimes you may feel confused all day about a decision. Then when you pray about it and go to bed, the right thing to do becomes clear. God is always there to give you advice, all day and all night. He never stops wanting to help. If you keep his Word in your heart and give your thoughts to him in prayer, he will make the right choices clear. Sometimes you just have to be quiet enough to hear what God has put in your heart. However, you have to be careful not to rely only on your emotions, but to check your choices against God's Word.

### Discussion Questions
- Why do you think time for Bible study and prayer is sometimes called "quiet time"?
- When have emotions (feelings) in your heart not matched what God's Word in your heart told you was right?

### Prayer Prompter
Thank you for wanting to counsel us. We need your guidance. Help us to listen carefully not just to our emotions, but to what you put in our hearts.

# God Is My Fortress
**Psalm 18:1-24**

### Memory Verse

*The Lord is my rock, my fortress and my deliverer; my God is my rock, in whom I take refuge. He is my shield and the horn of my salvation, my stronghold (Psalm 18:2).*

### Attention Grabber

Give the kids bed linens to make a fort indoors or outdoors. Read the devotion inside the fort. Explain that the word "fort" means a place that is strong against attacks during a war. In Bible times, some forts were made of rock.

### Living It

Did you know we're in a war? We're struggling against the devil and his evil forces. He is shooting bad situations, troubles, and temptations at us the same way soldiers would shoot burning arrows at an enemy (Ephesians 6:12, 16). In the battle against evil, God is our fortress. We can go to him, and he will protect us.

### Discussion Questions

◉ What are several ways God helps you resist the devil?

◉ In this psalm, David compares God to something from David's life. What is a symbol for God from your life? "God is like a _____ to me because he _____."

### Prayer Prompter

Thank you for being our fortress in this battle against the devil. Please protect us and keep us strong.

# Faithful
## Psalm 18:25-50

### Memory Verse

*To the faithful you show yourself faithful, to the blameless you show yourself blameless (Psalm 18:25).*

### Attention Grabber

Try to do something that the kids do better, such as yo-yo tricks, playing an instrument, or dribbling a basketball. When the kids offer some instruction to you, listen carefully. Emphasize that you paid close attention when you were trying to learn. Explain that as we try to learn to become more like God, we pay closer attention and we see more clearly how great he is.

### Living It

When we have faith in God, we believe he will keep his promises. As he does that, we see that he is faithful. James 4:8 promises, "Come near to God and he will come near to you." When we want to become more like him, we look at him closely. We study his Word and talk to him often. The more we do this, the more we realize who he is. God reveals himself to us. He is always faithful, blameless, and every other good thing, but the more we try to be like that ourselves, the more we notice that he is that way.

### Discussion Questions

- ◎ In what ways are you trying to become more like God?
- ◎ Are you blameless? Why or why not?

### Prayer Prompter

Thank you for the ways you reveal your holiness and faithfulness to us, Lord. Please help us to become more like you.

# Heavens Declare
**Psalm 19:1-13**

## Memory Verse
*The heavens declare the glory of God; the skies proclaim the work of his hands (Psalm 19:1).*

## Attention Grabber
If possible, watch a sunrise or sunset with your family. Give the kids colored chalk and blue construction paper so they can draw what they saw. Or, if you can't see the sunrise or sunset, just have the kids draw pictures of sunrises or sunsets they remember.

## Living It
If God wanted to, he could have made the sunrise or sunset like turning a lamp on and off—click, it's morning and click, it's night. But God does things in a grand way, doesn't he? All people have to do to know that there is a God is to walk outdoors and look up. It's almost as if God has written his signature in the sky!

## Discussion Questions
◉ Would you like to sleep under the stars? Why or why not?
◉ From what you see in nature, what do you think God's favorite color might be? What is yours?

## Prayer Prompter
We praise you for the beauty of your creations, Lord! Thank you for the sunrises and sunsets you give us to enjoy. Thank you for the sky and clouds. Thanks for the sun, moon, and stars.

# Pleasing in God's Sight
**Psalm 19:14**

## Memory Verse
*May the words of my mouth and the meditation of my heart be pleasing in your sight, O Lord, my Rock and my Redeemer (Psalm 19:14).*

## Attention Grabber
Have each child use a pencil to draw a simple outline of a mouth or heart. Then have him write the words of the verse inside or along the drawn lines.

## Living It
When you clean your room, do you ignore the space under the bed, leaving it cluttered and unswept because you don't expect anyone to look under there? It's easy to think that way about ourselves, too. Sometimes we may think that if we look good on the outside, no one will know what's on the inside. But actually, someone is looking inside. God sees our hearts, so they need to be as clean as the rest of us. We need to be careful about what we say, too. God is listening. In Matthew 12:36 Jesus says that "men will have to give account on the day of judgment for every careless word they have spoken."

## Discussion Questions
- Would you think and act differently than usual if you could always see Jesus standing in the room with you? Why or why not?
- What are some things you say and think that probably please God?

## Prayer Prompter
We love you and want to please you. Help our hearts and our words to be pure.

# Trust the Name
**Psalms 20, 21**

## Memory Verse

*Some trust in chariots and some in horses, but we trust in the name of the Lord our God (Psalm 20:7).*

## Attention Grabber

Come into the room wearing all kinds of protective gear, as if you were going into battle: a helmet, a shield (use a trash can lid for a shield), knee and elbow pads, bug spray, etc. Be creative! Tell the kids that you heard that a big bully moved into the neighborhood. Ask, "Do you think I am ready to fight?"

## Living It

Ancient armies thought they had a greater chance of winning if they had more chariots and horses than their enemies. But they were more likely to win if they were trusting God for the victory. In one battle that Gideon fought, God had him send most of his soldiers home! God wanted everyone to know that Gideon's army won because of God, not because the army was big (Judges 7:1-8). When he was a boy, David, who wrote Psalm 20, fought the giant Goliath. Before he did, he said, "It is not by sword or spear that the Lord saves; for the battle is the Lord's"(1 Samuel 17:47). We can accomplish whatever God asks if we trust in him. Instead of saying, "Where there's a will, there's a way," we can say, "When it's God's will, there's a way!"

## Discussion Questions

◉ What challenges have made you rely more on God?
◉ How could trusting God help you when you have to face a problem such as a bully at school? a tough test? a big fear?

## Prayer Prompter

Help us to trust you rather than just our own resources to help us accomplish your will.

# Family Faith
Psalm 22

## Memory Verse
*In you our fathers put their trust; they trusted and you delivered them (Psalm 22:4).*

## Attention Grabber
Beforehand, photocopy a family tree from page 265 for each family member or draw similar charts on construction paper and cut the paper into tree shapes. If you can, get reprints of family photos. Let the kids color the family trees, write the names in the blanks, and glue on the photos. Or have the kids draw portraits if photos aren't available. If desired, let the kids frame their family trees.

## Living It
Hearing about the faith of our ancestors can build our faith. We can learn from their wisdom and from their mistakes. What do you know about the faith of our family members? (Note: Share some of the ways God helped family members in the past. If there are not any believers in your family's history, mention ways that knowing God would have helped those family members. Be sure to tell about your own faith, too.) We can also build our faith by reading about people in the Bible who were faithful. Let's look at Hebrews 11:1–12:1 and see what happened to those people who had faith.

## Discussion Questions
◉ What do you hope your children will say about your faith someday?
◉ How are lives spent trusting God different from lives that aren't?

## Prayer Prompter
Thank you for putting us in this family, Lord. Thank you for the many ways you help our family.

 **Family Faith**

# My Shepherd
## Psalm 23*

### Memory Verse
*The Lord is my shepherd, I shall not be in want (Psalm 23:1).*

### Attention Grabber
Give each family member a Tootsie® Roll candy or piece of taffy to stretch and shape into a shepherd's staff (in the shape of a hook). Ask if the kids know the purposes of a shepherd's staff. (Shepherds might use their staffs to help them walk over rough ground, to pull sheep back into the flock, to fight off wild animals, etc.)

### Living It
Let's look in John 10:27, 28 and list characteristics of a shepherd and sheep. Jesus is like a shepherd to us in the ways he takes care of us and protects us. Jesus keeps us from being in want by giving us what we need to be fed, both physically and spiritually.

### Discussion Questions
◉ How are you like a sheep?
◉ How is Jesus like a shepherd to you?

### Prayer Prompter
Thank you for caring for us as a shepherd cares for sheep. Help us to follow where you lead.

*The next five devotions have the same reading to help your family memorize Psalm 23.*

# He Restores My Soul
**Psalm 23**

## Memory Verse
*He makes me lie down in green pastures, he leads me beside quiet waters, he restores my soul (Psalm 23:2, 3).*

## Attention Grabber
If you can, take a few minutes to lie down on a blanket in your backyard or at a nearby park. If it is winter, bundle up well first. You might even want to take time for a simple picnic lunch or dinner.

## Living It
Almost all families are very busy with many activities. Sometimes we can get so busy that we wear ourselves out physically, emotionally, mentally, and spiritually. If we spend time with Jesus in prayer, he restores us. That quiet time with him refreshes us the way we are refreshed when we lie down outside in a green field or on a riverbank. Jesus said, "Come to me, all you who are weary and burdened, and I will give you rest. Take my yoke upon you and learn from me, for I am gentle and humble in heart, and you will find rest for your souls" (Matthew 11:28, 29).

## Discussion Questions
◎ How have you felt when lying down outdoors?
◎ How did you feel the last time you had a long talk with the Lord?
◎ Besides prayer, what are some ways Jesus can restore you and give you rest?

## Prayer Prompter
Help us to slow down when we pray so we can feel the peace that you want to give us.

**He Restores My Soul**

7/23/08

# He Guides Me
## Psalm 23

### Memory Verse
*He guides me in paths of righteousness for his name's sake (Psalm 23:3).*

### Attention Grabber
Ask the kids what they do to keep from getting lost from you when they are shopping with you. Ask how this is similar to what they need to do to keep from getting spiritually lost from God.

### Living It
Do you ever think of your decisions as the beginnings of paths? Some paths are ones God wants you to be on, ones that will bring glory to him, and some aren't. If you stay close to the Lord by praying and studying the Bible, he warns you when you're headed the wrong way, and he gives you peace when you're headed the right way. He lets you know which way he wants you to go.

### Discussion Questions
- What are ways that God guides you?
- Discuss where each of the following paths could lead: being rebellious, using illegal drugs, serving others, telling a friend about Jesus, looking at inappropriate cable channels or web sites, etc. Which of these could be paths of righteousness?

### Prayer Prompter
Please help us to follow your guidance, and keep us close to you.

# Through the Valley
**Psalm 23**

## Memory Verse
*Even though I walk through the valley of the shadow of death, I will fear no evil, for you are with me; your rod and your staff, they comfort me (Psalm 23:4).*

## Attention Grabber
Let the kids watch sand fall through a sand timer or watch salt pour through a piece of paper shaped into a funnel and placed in a jar. Explain that everyone has a limited number of days on the earth.

## Living It
All of us will die sometime, and none of us knows exactly when that time will be. Many people fear death, but believers can face it bravely because Jesus will be with them. If you believe in Jesus, you can trust that he will give you comfort and bring you to heaven. He will also help you to bear sorrow when your loved ones die.

## Discussion Questions
◉ Have you ever felt like you were walking through a dark time in your life in which you needed Jesus?
◉ When have you felt alone? Were you really alone then? (No. Your emotions may make you feel that way, but in Matthew 28:20 Jesus promises that he will be with you always.)

## Prayer Prompter
Please help us not to be afraid of our deaths or the deaths of those we love. Help us to trust that you will always be with us and that you will help us through whatever the future holds.

# My Cup Overflows
### Psalm 23

## Memory Verse

*You prepare a table before me in the presence of my enemies. You anoint my head with oil; my cup overflows (Psalm 23:5).*

## Attention Grabber

Place a cup inside a soup bowl in front of each child. Slowly pour a drink the kids like into each cup. Each time you fill a cup, keep pouring until the cup overflows. Explain that this is like the love and blessings that God pours into our lives.

## Living It

God is good to us even when others aren't. He blesses us even when people around us don't want good things to happen to us. He gives us even more than we need.

## Discussion Questions

◉ What blessings do you appreciate most?
◉ In what parts of your life has God given you even more than you need?

## Prayer Prompter

Thank you for the love and blessings you pour into our lives.

# Bright Future
## Psalm 23

### Memory Verse
*Surely goodness and love will follow me all the days of my life, and I will dwell in the house of the Lord forever (Psalm 23:6).*

### Attention Grabber
Look into a pair of binoculars (or two paper cups with the bottoms removed). Ask the kids, "If I could look into your future through a pair of magic binoculars, do you know what I would see?" Emphasize that God promises believers goodness, love, and a place in God's house. If you know it, sing the Audio Adrenaline song "Big House" from their *Don't Censor Me* album.

### Living It
If we have faith in God, we have a lot to be optimistic about when we think about what lies ahead of us. No matter what difficulties we face, God will be with us. That means that even when situations or people are bad, we can think about God's goodness. Even if people aren't always loving to us, we can feel God's love. And even if we don't like a situation we're in, we know it will last only a little while. We can trust that in the end, we will get to be with God forever!

### Discussion Questions
◎ In what ways will goodness and love follow you?
◎ Why do you want to go to heaven?

### Prayer Prompter
Thank you for giving us a great future. We look forward to being with you in heaven.

# Rebellious Ways

**Psalms 24:1–25:7**

### Memory Verse

*Remember not the sins of my youth and my rebellious ways; according to your love remember me, for you are good, O Lord (Psalm 25:7).*

### Attention Grabber

Dress like a rebellious teen. (For example, wear the waist of your pants on your hips, or put a clip-on or magnetic earring in your nose.) Begin the devotion with a silly sneer on your face. Fold your arms and look toward the ceiling. Ask, "Do I look like a rebel?" (Be prepared for the kids to laugh at you!)

### Living It

You may be tempted to rebel against authority figures, especially as you get older. God doesn't want you to give in to the temptation to rebel against your parents and church leaders because he put those people in your life to help you. God has given your parents authority over you to teach you. They're the people who care about you the most. Most friendships are temporary, but your parents will always love you. But if you do rebel, if you trust that Jesus took the punishment for your sins, he will forgive you when you ask him for forgiveness.

### Discussion Questions

- What are reasons that some kids rebel?
- What temptations will you probably face more in your teen years than at any other time in your life?

### Prayer Prompter

Please help us not rebel against you or those you have put in our lives to guide us.

**Rebellious Ways**          **43**

# Release From Snares

## Memory Verse

*My eyes are ever on the Lord, for only he will release my feet from the snare (Psalm 25:15).*

## Attention Grabber

Give family members magnets that they can glue to the back of unused mousetraps to make message holders for the door of your refrigerator (make sure the kids do not play with the traps). Or make a simple trap by tying a string to a stick and then using the stick to prop up a box. Show how a person might catch an animal by pulling the string when the animal comes for the food placed under the box. Discuss other ways hunters trap animals. Emphasize that when traps catch animals, the animals can't get free without help.

## Living It

Sometimes we are like animals that are about to step in a trap. The devil is trying to trip us up. He wants to trap us in sin so we will be sidetracked from doing God's will and so that we'll be miserable. When we start to get trapped by sin, we need to ask God for help as quickly as possible. We can't get out on our own without God. Even if we get stuck in the devil's traps, we can trust God to free us from them. All we have to do is call for God and he will give us a way out of the trap.

## Discussion Questions

◎ How is sin like a trap?
◎ In what ways can God free us from the devil's traps?

## Prayer Prompter

Please help us stay away from the devil's traps.

# My Light

## Memory Verse
*The Lord is my light and my salvation—whom shall I fear? The Lord is the stronghold of my life—of whom shall I be afraid? (Psalm 27:1).*

## Attention Grabber
Ask the kids if they remember being afraid at night when they were little and coming to your bedroom. Have them all pile into your bed with you and pull up the covers. Turn off the lights and discuss how sometimes when it's dark, objects in the room can look more frightening than they do in the light. Then flip on the lights and point out how the light shows that there is nothing to be afraid of in the room. Sing a praise song about light if you know one.

## Living It
In John 8:12, Jesus said, "I am the light of the world. Whoever follows me will never walk in darkness, but will have the light of life." Jesus' light gets rid of dark sin and brightens up parts of life that could be frightening. If we believe in him, he gives us salvation so we don't need to fear what will happen to us after we die. Jesus takes away all of our reasons to fear.

## Discussion Questions
◉ What are some of your fears, and how can Jesus help you with them?
◉ In what ways is Jesus a light in your life?

## Prayer Prompter
Thank you for being our light and helping us not be afraid.

# Joy in the Morning

**Psalms 29, 30**

## Memory Verse

*For his anger lasts only a moment, but his favor lasts a lifetime; weeping may remain for a night, but rejoicing comes in the morning (Psalm 30:5).*

## Attention Grabber

Cover a box of facial tissues with gift wrap or fabric, leaving an opening for the hole where the tissues are pulled out. Mention that sometimes we might cry or feel sad when we've done something wrong, but after we say we are sorry and our punishment is finished, we can feel good again. Have the kids write the verse on index cards and glue the cards onto the sides of the box.

## Living It

When we know we've done something that God doesn't like, it's painful to admit it. But God's anger only lasts a moment. His forgiveness lasts forever! When we repent and tell God how sorry we are, he is like the prodigal son's father who welcomed his son back with open arms (Luke 15:11-24). We don't have to spend our lives being full of sin and miserable while running from God. We can repent and experience the joy of being forgiven.

## Discussion Questions

⦿ How is God's love for you like your parents' love for you?
⦿ Why do your tears turn to joy when you repent?

## Prayer Prompter

Help us to stop doing things that anger you. Please forgive us for our sins. Help us to experience the joy repentance brings. Help us to trust you to forgive us as you have promised.

# God Sees My Pain

## Memory Verse
*I will be glad and rejoice in your love, for you saw my affliction and knew the anguish of my soul (Psalm 31:7).*

## Attention Grabber
Ask the kids to finish this saying: "Sticks and stones may break my bones ..." (but words will never hurt me). Emphasize that words can hurt even more than sticks. Hurt feelings can be as painful or even more painful than physical injuries. When we hurt emotionally or physically, we can go to God for help.

## Living It
Jesus understands when we are hurt and sad because he has been hurt, too. At Gethsemane he said, "My soul is overwhelmed with sorrow to the point of death" (Mark 14:34). He understands when we are tempted because he "has been tempted in every way, just as we are—yet was without sin" (Hebrews 4:15). Even if other people don't see when we are hurting, God does. He cares when we hurt, and he wants us to let ourselves feel his love for us. Feeling God's love can heal our pain.

## Discussion Questions
- What makes you sad that is too small to talk about with God? (That's a trick question because God cares about every detail of your life.)
- What soothes physical pain, such as a sunburn? How does God soothe your pain when your feelings are hurt?

## Prayer Prompter
Thank you for loving us. Thank you for understanding when we hurt. Please help us open up to you and let you heal our pain.

# Disappearing Sin
## Psalm 32:1-7

### Memory Verse

*Blessed is the man whose sin the Lord does not count against him and in whose spirit is no deceit (Psalm 32:2).*

### Attention Grabber

Use chalk on a sidewalk to show the kids how to count with tally marks. Let them draw some tally marks. Ask them to think about how many marks there might be on the sidewalk if all of our sins were counted there. Pour water on the marks. As the tally marks disappear, explain that God wants to wash away our sins.

### Living It

Deceit is dishonesty or trickery. God doesn't want us to try to trick him, others, or even ourselves into thinking we haven't sinned. He wants us to be honest, admit our sins, and let him wash them away. Then we can feel happy and pure.

### Discussion Questions

- How can you be blessed when God takes away your sins? (your guilt can be removed, you'll be able to go to heaven, feel God's love, etc.)
- What do you really deserve for your sins? If you believe in Jesus, why won't you get what you deserve? (Romans 6:23 says we deserve death but we don't get that because Jesus died for us.)

### Prayer Prompter

Thank you for blessing us with your forgiveness when we repent. Thank you for loving us enough to send your Son to take the punishment for our sins.

**Disappearing Sin**

# Don't Be a Mule
**Psalm 32:8-11**

### Memory Verse

*Do not be like the horse or the mule, which have no understanding but must be controlled by bit and bridle or they will not come to you (Psalm 32:9).*

### Attention Grabber

If your kids are not too heavy for you, let them have a "horseback" ride on your back. Explain that a rider controls a horse by pulling on reins attached to a bit in the horse's mouth.

### Living It

God doesn't want to force us to do right. He has given us the freedom to make our own choices. He wants us to learn from him and to obey him because he loves us. The choice to follow God is always the best way. We need to gain understanding to know how to follow him and to be able to recognize when we're on a wrong path.

### Discussion Questions

◉ Who are some Bible people that God almost had to force to obey him? (Moses, Balaam, Jonah, Paul, etc.)
◉ How can you gain understanding about what God wants you to do?

### Prayer Prompter

Please help us to be humble, so that we will obey you without being forced.

# His Word Is True
## Psalm 33:1-5

### Memory Verse
*For the word of the Lord is right and true; he is faithful in all he does (Psalm 33:4).*

### Attention Grabber
Tell the kids you are giving them a simple true-false test. Draw a line down the middle of a piece of paper. Write "true" on one side and "false" on the other. Hand a Bible to one of the kids and ask, "True or false?" Have her place it on the "true" side.

### Living It
Second Timothy 3:16 says, "All Scripture is God-breathed." That means the whole Bible comes from God. You can trust God to be faithful. He will keep the promises he has made in the Bible. His most important promise is to save all those who believe in Jesus. You can trust him to be faithful to save you if you believe in Jesus. (If your child seems ready to trust Jesus, see page 270 for help.)

### Discussion Questions
◎ What does it mean to "keep your word"?
◎ What promises of God have you seen fulfilled in your life?

### Prayer Prompter
Please help us to trust you to keep all of your promises. Help us to have faith that whoever trusts Jesus as Savior will be saved.

# His Plans Stand Firm

**Psalm 33:6-11**

## Memory Verse

*But the plans of the Lord stand firm forever, the purposes of his heart through all generations (Psalm 33:11).*

## Attention Grabber

Make fun family plans for an upcoming weekend and write them on the calendar. Discuss the difference between tentative plans and firm plans.

## Living It

The Lord has firm plans to seek and save the lost; that's why Jesus came to earth (Luke 19:10). Second Peter 3:9 says the Lord doesn't want anyone to perish. Salvation (saving people from hell) has always been his goal. It is his goal now, and it will be his goal in the future. Hebrews 6:17 says his purpose is unchanging. God has other firm plans too, such as to help you to become more like Jesus (Romans 8:29). When it seems like it is taking a long time for God to finish helping you become like Jesus, don't get discouraged. The Bible promises that "he who began a good work in you will carry it on to completion until the day of Christ Jesus" (Philippians 1:6).

## Discussion Questions

- What are some of the plans God may have for your life? If you don't know, how can you find out what they are?
- What do you think are some plans God might have for your day today or tomorrow?

## Prayer Prompter

Help us to know what your plans are for us, and help us to cooperate. Thank you for being so firm that we can rely on you. Please use us to fulfill your plans for all to be saved.

# God Watches
## Psalm 33:12-22

### Memory Verse
*From heaven the Lord looks down and sees all mankind; from his dwelling place he watches all who live on earth (Psalm 33:13, 14).*

### Attention Grabber
Have the kids draw trees the way they look if you stand on the ground and look up at them. Then have them draw trees the way they would look if you were looking down on them from a helicopter or tall building. Explain that the viewpoint from which you see things is called your "perspective."

### Living It
Have you ever heard the expression, "You can't see the forest for the trees"? Sometimes it's hard for us to see the whole picture because we are so close to the situation. God has a much better perspective. He can see everything around us, everything before us and after us. It is important to follow his guidance because he knows more about our situations than we do. He understands what it is like to be on earth going through the situations we do because Jesus lived here and was "tempted in every way" (Hebrews 4:15).

### Discussion Questions
◉ What is the highest you have ever been off the ground? How did being up high change how things looked to you?
◉ Does it comfort you or worry you to know God is watching you? Why?

### Prayer Prompter
Thank you for watching over us, Lord. Help us always to trust that you know what's best for us.

# From All My Fears

## Memory Verse

*I sought the Lord, and he answered me; he delivered me from all my fears (Psalm 34:4).*

## Attention Grabber

Let the kids make individual pizza "scaredy cats." Spread tomato sauce on toasted English muffins. Top with shredded cheese. Arrange black olive slices as eyes. Cut other olive slices in half and use the halves for the nose and both sides of the mouth. Cut pepperoni slices into triangles for ears and strips for whiskers. Or decorate English muffins with marmalade, raisins, and pretzel stick "whiskers."

## Living It

President Franklin D. Roosevelt once said that we have nothing to fear but fear itself. Sometimes fear can cause us greater trouble than the problems themselves! God hasn't given us a spirit of fear (2 Timothy 1:7, *KJV*). What does the expression "paralyzed with fear" mean? (When you're afraid, sometimes you can't even move.) God does not want our lives to be paralyzed with fear. He doesn't want us to be so anxious that we stop doing everything. The devil wants us to be afraid so we won't do what God wants. But God wants us to go to him when we're afraid so he can free us from our fears.

## Discussion Questions

◉ How can fears get in the way of what God wants you to do?
◉ What fear has God helped you overcome?

## Prayer Prompter

Please take away our fears, Lord. Don't let the devil paralyze us and keep us from doing your will. Help us trust you in whatever situations frighten us.

# Radiant Faces
## Psalm 34:5-9

## Memory Verse

*Those who look to him are radiant; their faces are never covered with shame (Psalm 34:5).*

## Attention Grabber

If you have one, show a glow-in-the-dark object to the kids. Explain how the object has to absorb light before it can give off light in the dark. Emphasize that when we spend time with God, our lives can reflect his light.

## Living It

Have you ever been able to tell when a person has recently been out in the sun? If so, how did you know? (by seeing that person's tan or sunburn) When Moses talked with God, his friends could tell right away because his face was actually glowing (Exodus 34:30). Even though our faces may not literally glow when we talk with God, people can tell. How does it show in our faces? When we have a relationship with God and talk to him on a regular basis, we have the joy that comes from knowing God's love. We are able to make better decisions and handle hard situations with a sense of peace that nonbelievers don't have.

## Discussion Questions

- When was the last time you had a heart-to-heart talk with the Lord?
- How does the condition of your relationship with God show in your face? in your actions?

## Prayer Prompter

Please remind us to look to you in every situation. Help us to spend enough time with you that our cares melt away and we feel so joyful that it shows in our faces.

# Nothing Lacking
**Psalm 34:10-16**

## Memory Verse
*The lions may grow weak and hungry, but those who seek the Lord lack no good thing (Psalm 34:10).*

## Attention Grabber
Let the kids finger paint pictures of lions on paper plates with instant banana pudding or vanilla pudding dyed with yellow food coloring.

## Living It
Lions seem very strong, but even they can grow weak if they don't have what they need. If we seek God, we will have what we need. We don't have to grow weak because Jesus gives us his energy (Colossians 1:29). We can remind ourselves of Philippians 4:13, which says, "I can do everything through him who gives me strength."

## Discussion Questions
◉ What do you need? Let's pray about those things.
◉ Do you feel strong or weak? Why?

## Prayer Prompter
Help us to look for you, God. Please take care of us and give us what we need. Help us to rely on you for our strength.

# Feeling Crushed
## Psalm 34:17, 18

## Memory Verse

*The Lord is close to the brokenhearted and saves those who are crushed in spirit (Psalm 34:18).*

## Attention Grabber

Give each family member a sealable plastic bag partially filled with shelled peanuts (not dry-roasted). As they crush the peanuts with the back of a spoon or a hammer, explain that sometimes trials and sins make our hearts feel broken and crushed. When the nuts are crushed to the point of being peanut butter, spread the nuts in a heart shape on a cracker for each person. Or give the kids hard-boiled eggs and have them crack the shells on the table before peeling the eggs. Emphasize that sometimes the "hard knocks" of life make us feel crushed and broken. Explain that those who turn to Jesus are saved, and their heartaches are healed.

## Living It

Many people who don't know God think that God is distant and unfeeling and doesn't care about their problems. But God does care! When bad things happen to us that make us feel broken and crushed, God is there with us. He is the one who can heal our pain.

## Discussion Questions

◉ How has God helped when you have felt brokenhearted?
◉ Do you know people who are hurting and need Jesus? How could you help them?

## Prayer Prompter

Please heal our heartaches and help us to remember times when you have done that for us in the past. Help us to tell others openly about how you have helped us so they will turn to you when their hearts are broken, too.

Feeling Crushed

# From All Troubles

## Memory Verse

*A righteous man may have many troubles, but the Lord delivers him from them all (Psalm 34:19).*

## Attention Grabber

Make popcorn. Have the kids listen for when the popping starts and stops. Emphasize that troubles pop up for Christians like they do for everyone, but the Lord delivers us from them.

## Living It

John 16:33 says that in this world we will have trouble. How do you feel when you have troubles? James 1:2 says to consider it pure joy whenever you face trials. That isn't easy, is it? It can be helpful to remember that the troubles are temporary. God will deliver us from them. In the meantime, it is good to try to see the ways the trials are helping us grow. First Peter 1:7 says that these trials come so that we'll have genuine faith; we'll see how God has been faithful to help us through the trials.

## Discussion Questions

- ◉ What troubles has the Lord delivered you from already? Which are you still experiencing right now?
- ◉ What are some reasons the Lord may not take our trials away immediately?

## Prayer Prompter

Help us to trust that when you let us go through troubles, you are helping us grow. Help us to rely on you to get us through our troubles and to deliver us from them when your purposes have been accomplished.

# Love High as the Sky
**Psalm 36**

## Memory Verse
*Your love, O Lord, reaches to the heavens, your faithfulness to the skies (Psalm 36:5).*

## Attention Grabber
Remind the kids that when a pilot skywrites, the message looks like it was written with shaving cream. Tell them to imagine that a can of shaving cream is a skywriting plane. Let them use the shaving cream to write "God loves me high as the sky!" on the lawn, and then rinse off the message with a hose. If you can't go outdoors, let them write it in the bathtub or on the bathtub tile wall, and then rinse off the message before it dries.

## Living It
It's hard to imagine how much God loves us, isn't it? There is evidence all around us if we look at the blessings in our lives and the ways he has helped us. John 3:16 says that God loved us so much that he gave his one and only Son so that whoever would believe in him would have eternal life. God loves us enough to want us to live with him forever, and he loves us enough that he let his Son suffer and die for our sins. Paul prayed that people would let Jesus in their hearts and "grasp how wide and long and high and deep is the love of Christ" (Ephesians 3:18). God's love is as high as the sky—and higher!

## Discussion Questions
◎ When do you feel God's love?
◎ What are some ways God has shown his love to you?

## Prayer Prompter
Thank you for loving us all of the time. We love you, too. Thanks for listening to every prayer, no matter what time of day or night we call on you. Thank you for faithfully answering every prayer in the way that is best for us.

# Desires of My Heart
## Psalm 37:1-4

## Memory Verse

*Delight yourself in the Lord and he will give you the desires of your heart (Psalm 37:4).*

## Attention Grabber

Have each family member draw a heart on a piece of paper. Ask them to draw their most heartfelt desires within the hearts.

## Living It

How do you feel when you are delighted? (thrilled, happy) Have you ever been delighted when a friend called or came to see you? God wants us to feel delighted by our time with him. As we become closer to God and trust in him, we learn more about what he desires for our lives. Then we begin to want those same things for ourselves because we realize that God always knows what is best for us. God promises to give those who delight themselves in him their most heartfelt desires.

## Discussion Questions

- ◎ What is the greatest thing that has happened to you this week that you can tell God about?
- ◎ Why might our desires not always be things that God would want to give us?

## Prayer Prompter

Help us to be good friends to you as you are to us. Help our desires to become more like yours. Thank you for making us feel great when we pray or worship you.

# Be Still and Wait
### Psalm 37:5-20

## Memory Verse

*Be still before the Lord and wait patiently for him; do not fret when men succeed in their ways, when they carry out their wicked schemes (Psalm 37:7).*

## Attention Grabber

Have a simple race in which everyone takes off running as soon as you ring a bell, honk a horn, or wave a flag. Ask the kids what it means to "jump the gun."

## Living It

When we have asked God to guide us, why is it a bad idea to go ahead with our own plans before listening to him? (We might get busy doing something that isn't God's will.) In Matthew 7:7, Jesus promised, "Ask and it will be given to you; seek and you will find; knock and the door will be opened to you." We need to be patient until God answers us. While we are waiting, we should continue to read his Word, pray, and obey his commands.

## Discussion Questions

◉ What are some reasons God might delay answering a prayer?
◉ What are some prayers you are waiting for God to answer?

## Prayer Prompter

Please help us to be patient for you to answer our prayers, Lord. Help us not to go ahead without you.

**Be Still and Wait**

# Be Generous
## Psalm 37:21-31

### Memory Verse

*The wicked borrow and do not repay, but the righteous give generously (Psalm 37:21).*

### Attention Grabber

Write the memory verse with a permanent marker on a clean, empty jar. Let the kids decorate the jar with paint pens or permanent markers. Have them think of a charity or a family that is struggling financially that they would like to help. Make a goal of filling the jar with cash by a particular date. Discuss ways they can earn money to give.

### Living It

God wants us to be givers instead of takers. Sometimes we may need to borrow, but it is wrong not to return what we borrow. Doing that is similar to stealing. It inconveniences people and can make them think we don't care about their feelings.

### Discussion Questions

◉ Have you borrowed toys, books, or anything else from others that you need to return?
◉ What makes you want to be generous with your offerings to church? with your help to the poor? with your gifts to family and friends?

### Prayer Prompter

Please help us to be careful to return what we have borrowed. Thank you for being generous to us. Please help us to be generous to others.

# Observe the Upright
## Psalms 37:32–38:22

### Memory Verse

*Consider the blameless, observe the upright; there is a future for the man of peace (Psalm 37:37).*

### Attention Grabber

Give everyone note cards, pens, and envelopes. Have each family member write a short, encouraging note to someone from church or someone else the family knows and respects. Each family member should write why he respects or admires the chosen person and express thanks for the good things that person has done.

### Living It

It is good to learn from people who are upright, who make good decisions, and who do the right things. Watching these people and paying attention to what they do can help us see how to be more like Jesus. But most of all, we need to focus on Jesus himself and follow his example.

### Discussion Questions

- Everyone sins, so how can someone be blameless? (Jesus can take his sins away.)
- Who do we know who can be good examples to us of how Jesus wants us to live? What can we learn about Jesus by observing them?

### Prayer Prompter

Thank you for the people you have put in our lives who show us how to follow you. Help us learn from them.

# Wait Patiently
## Psalms 39:1–40:1

## Memory Verse
*I waited patiently for the Lord; he turned to me and heard my cry (Psalm 40:1).*

## Attention Grabber
Jingle the car keys or act out some other behavior that you do when you're trying to rush everyone to get out the door. Ask, "Am I waiting patiently?" When they answer no, ask, "What are some things you do when you're impatient?"

## Living It
Sometimes we might feel impatient with God. When we ask him for something, we want it at that moment. We need to trust God's timing and wisdom. God knows what we need and he will give it to us when we need it. If we can remember this, we will be able to have more patience as we wait for God's answers.

## Discussion Questions
- ◉ What are some blessings in your life that were worth the wait?
- ◉ Why do you think God makes us wait sometimes? Why do you think God says no sometimes?

## Prayer Prompter
Thank you for loving us enough to listen to our prayers and answer us. Please help us to wait patiently for the guidance and blessings we need.

# Out of the Slimy Pit
## Psalm 40:2-4

### Memory Verse

*He lifted me out of the slimy pit, out of the mud and mire; he set my feet on a rock and gave me a firm place to stand (Psalm 40:2).*

### Attention Grabber

With the kids' help, make "slime" according to the directions on page 269. Or have the kids stand on a large rock or another firm surface to recite the memory verse.

### Living It

When we try to walk in mud or slime, sometimes we get stuck and have trouble moving forward. Sometimes we slip around so much that we can't get secure footing. Sin is like that. Sin can get our emotions and thoughts tangled up in bad feelings and bad ideas. Sin makes it hard for us to seek God and to move toward obeying him. God wants to pull us out of that mess. He wants us to be able to stand firm. He wants us to know right from wrong so that we can make good choices. Like the house built on a rock, God wants us to be able to stand strong when the storms of life come. Slime is disgusting. People are usually ashamed of their sins because sins are disgusting, too. God wants to wash away all of our filth.

### Discussion Questions

◎ Who do you know whose life changed dramatically after that person accepted the Lord?

◎ What kind of life do you think you would have without Jesus?

### Prayer Prompter

Thank you for wanting to pull us out of the filth of sin. Help us always to stand firm with you.

# Many Wonders

## Memory Verse

*Many, O Lord my God, are the wonders you have done. The things you planned for us no one can recount to you; were I to speak and tell of them, they would be too many to declare (Psalm 40:5).*

## Attention Grabber

Ask each family member to choose a Bible person to pretend to be. Tell each to keep her chosen Bible character a secret. Then ask each person what God has done for her (she should answer as if she were the Bible character). Let the rest of the family guess who each character is. Or give everyone a folder to decorate as a journal in which to write answers to prayers and other experiences of God's involvement in each of their lives.

## Living It

God has plans for everyone. We all need to have a close relationship with him so we will know what he wants to do in our lives. If we are actively letting God lead our lives daily, he will do great things. It's a good idea to write down the special things God does for us so that we won't forget them later.

## Discussion Questions

- What are some of your prayers that God has answered?
- What is something you've done because it was what God wanted?

## Prayer Prompter

We praise you for the great things you have done in our lives. Thanks for hearing and answering our prayers. Thanks for guiding us and helping us to follow you.

# Doing God's Will
## Psalm 40:6-8

### Memory Verse
*"I desire to do your will, O my God; your law is within my heart"*
*(Psalm 40:8).*

### Attention Grabber
Hold a camera and ask if anyone knows what pictures are on the film inside. If you would like, take a picture. Emphasize that eventually what is inside the camera will come out for everyone to see. What we desire in our hearts will come out in our actions.

### Living It
When we do what God's law requires, we show that his law is written on our hearts (Romans 2:13-15). If we follow him, God uses our lives to teach others. In 2 Corinthians 3:3, Paul says, "You show that you are a letter from Christ, the result of our ministry, written not with ink but with the Spirit of the living God, not on tablets of stone but on tablets of human hearts." We can show others the result of Jesus' ministry to us by trying to live like Christ. The way we act on the outside shows the difference that Christ has made in our lives on the inside.

### Discussion Questions
- Which commands are easy for you to keep? Which are more difficult?
- Why do you keep God's commands?
- What in your actions might show others that you follow Christ?

### Prayer Prompter
Help us to do what we know in our hearts is right. Help us to obey your Word.

# Don't Hide It
## Psalms 40:9–41:13

### Memory Verse
*I do not hide your righteousness in my heart; I speak of your faithfulness and salvation. I do not conceal your love and your truth from the great assembly (Psalm 40:10).*

### Attention Grabber
Beforehand, look around the room in which you will have this devotion and hide four or five items in that room that the kids use often. (For example, hide the remote control from the TV room, or silverware from the breakfast table.) When it's time for the devotion, have the kids guess what is missing. Let them find the items. Emphasize that if things are hidden so we can't find them, we won't be able to use them when we need them. Everyone needs Jesus. We need to help people find him by telling them about him.

### Living It
If we have a close relationship with God, he does such great things in our lives that we can't help but share them with other people. We want to tell how faithfully he keeps his promises. We want to share how happy we are to know we'll go to heaven because of Jesus. We want to tell others that they can feel his love, too. We want to help them know the truth that has helped us.

### Discussion Questions
◉ How does feeling God's love help you?
◉ What keeps you from telling others about Jesus? How can you overcome that?

### Prayer Prompter
Please give us opportunities to share your love and truth with others.

# As the Deer
## Psalm 42:1-10

### Memory Verse
*As the deer pants for streams of water, so my soul pants for you, O God (Psalm 42:1).*

### Attention Grabber
Show the kids a picture of a deer if you have one (for example, a snapshot or encyclopedia picture). Ask the kids if they have ever seen a real deer. Talk about what kinds of activities might make a deer thirsty. If you know the praise song based on Psalm 42:1, sing it.

### Living It
What is the thirstiest you have ever been? Have you ever longed for God like that? It's possible to need him and not even realize that's the problem. If you are feeling discouraged, cranky, or lonely, you're probably thirsty for God!

### Discussion Questions
◎ How could you describe thirst to someone who has never felt it?
◎ How can your thirsty soul get a drink?

### Prayer Prompter
Please help us recognize when we're thirsty for you and to go to you. Remind us to pray and read the Bible. Help us go to church regularly.

# Hope in God
## Psalms 42:11–43:5

### Memory Verse

*Why are you downcast, O my soul? Why so disturbed within me? Put your hope in God, for I will yet praise him, my Savior and my God (Psalm 42:11).*

### Attention Grabber

Make a frowning face on the table out of two coins and a string or any other objects you have handy. Use the coins for eyes and the string for the frown. Explain that when we feel bad, if we pray and praise God, we will begin to feel better. Change the frown to a smile. If you know it, sing the song that is based on Psalm 42:11.

### Living It

When we're down, what should we do? Praise the Lord! Often what has gotten us in a bad mood is thinking about what's bad about ourselves, others, or our situation. Instead, if we think about God's goodness and perfection, it's like opening drapes and letting sunshine fill a dark room.

### Discussion Questions

◉ What is your favorite praise song? How does it make you feel when you hear or sing it?

◉ What hope do you have in God that can cheer you? What happy ending does God have for those who follow him?

### Prayer Prompter

When we feel down, help us remember to put our hope in you. Help us to praise you and let you lift our spirits.

# Be Still and Know
## Psalms 44–46

### Memory Verse
*"Be still, and know that I am God; I will be exalted among the nations, I will be exalted in the earth"* (Psalm 46:10).

### Attention Grabber
If you have Steven Curtis Chapman's *Speechless* album, play "Be Still and Know." See who can be quiet the longest without moving.

### Living It
Are there things in your life that keep you too busy? Have you ever felt too busy to pray? Jesus had a lot to accomplish in only three years of ministry on the earth, but still he took time to pray. Do you say your prayers quickly and then jump up to do something without listening for an answer? If you take the time to be still and wait for God, he will guide you and help you. He has the power to do whatever you need.

### Discussion Questions
- Is there anything you are trying to do that you ought to rely on God to do instead?
- What is a benefit of slowing down to listen to God?

### Prayer Prompter
Help us not to jump up and get busy rather than waiting on you, Lord. Help us to have faith that you have the power to take care of us and our needs. Help us to listen carefully for your direction and remember not to run ahead without you.

# Clap and Shout
## Psalms 47, 48

### Memory Verse
*Clap your hands, all you nations; shout to God with cries of joy (Psalm 47:1).*

### Attention Grabber
Play a clapping game in which one person claps out a rhythm of up to five beats. The next person claps that rhythm and adds up to five beats more. Continue around the circle until someone can't remember the pattern. Then clap as you sing a praise song that has a strong beat.

### Living It
Clapping is a way to praise God. You could think of it as a way to applaud God. Clapping is also something we do when we celebrate. When we clap and sing praise songs to God, we celebrate God's goodness.

### Discussion Questions
- When have people clapped for you? How did you feel? How do you think God feels when we clap for him?
- How do you feel when you are clapping along while singing a praise song?

### Prayer Prompter
We praise you, Lord! It gives us joy to think about how great you are. Thanks for giving us clapping as a way to praise you.

# Can't Take It With You
## Psalm 49

### Memory Verse

*Do not be overawed when a man grows rich, when the splendor of his house increases; for he will take nothing with him when he dies, his splendor will not descend with him (Psalm 49:16, 17).*

### Attention Grabber

Place an empty suitcase on the table. Ask, "If you knew you would die today, what would you pack to take with you?" Explain that it's a bit of a trick question, because you can't take anything on earth with you when you die.

### Living It

Some people are very impressed by riches and treat the wealthy as if they are more important than anyone else. God wants us to treat everyone well. He doesn't want us to be impressed by wealth. Money won't matter at all after we die. James 2:1-9 says not to treat a rich man who comes to church wearing a gold ring and fine clothes better than someone wearing shabby clothes and, "if you show favoritism, you sin."

### Discussion Questions

◉ Luke 12:13-21 emphasizes that instead of storing up belongings for ourselves, we should be "rich toward God." What does that mean?

◉ How are you rich in ways that will make an impact on others that will last even after you are gone?

### Prayer Prompter

Please help us to treat all people equally well. Help us to remember how temporary wealth is.

**Can't Take It With You**

# It's All God's
## Psalm 50

### Memory Verse
*"For every animal of the forest is mine, and the cattle on a thousand hills" (Psalm 50:10).*

### Attention Grabber
Tell the kids that everything in the world belongs to God, even cows. Give everyone a glass of chocolate milk or a brown cow (root beer with a scoop of vanilla ice cream). For fun, ask, "Did these come from cows that were brown?" (We don't know what color the cows were.) Emphasize that no matter what color the cows were, they belong to God like everything else does.

### Living It
God owns everything in the entire world. He doesn't need our tithes and offerings. He wants them because they show him we're thankful and they show that we realize our money really belongs to God. We're just stewards, or managers, of his money.

### Discussion Questions
- What's the difference between an owner and a steward? (A steward takes care of what belongs to an owner.)
- In addition to giving money, how can we give back to God some of the blessings he has given to us?

### Prayer Prompter
Please help us remember that the money and belongings we have actually belong to you. Thank you for trusting us with them.

# A Pure Heart
**Psalm 51:1-11**

## Memory Verse
*Create in me a pure heart, O God, and renew a steadfast spirit within me (Psalm 51:10).*

## Attention Grabber
Rub scraps of soap across a grater and then let each family member mold the soap shavings into hearts. Moisten the shavings with a few drops of water, if necessary.

## Living It
We need to ask God to wash the sin out of our hearts daily. Every morning the Lord will show us mercy and compassion (Lamentations 3:22, 23). We also need to ask him to help us be steadfast in our commitment to him. "Steadfast" means firm and determined.

## Discussion Questions
◎ What kinds of things keep your heart from being pure? What can you do to avoid or get rid of these things?
◎ Why do we need God's help for us to be steadfast?

## Prayer Prompter
Thank you for loving us all of the time and forgiving us. Please cleanse our hearts and help us to be steadfast in following you.

**A Pure Heart**

# Restore My Joy

## Memory Verse
*Restore to me the joy of your salvation and grant me a willing spirit, to sustain me (Psalm 51:12).*

## Attention Grabber
Tell the kids how you felt when you first accepted Jesus. Ask those who have accepted him how they felt when they first understood how to be saved and believed that they would be. (If any of your children seems ready to trust Jesus, turn to page 270 for help.)

## Living It
When people first believe that they can receive God's forgiveness through accepting Jesus' sacrifice, they are extremely happy. This joy about being saved helps new Christians to be willing to make changes in their lives. It helps them want to follow God's commands. Unfortunately, sometimes that zeal fades and it becomes harder to follow God. From time to time, we need to ask God to renew our excitement about our salvation and to help us to keep following him. Romans 12:11 says, "Never be lacking in zeal, but keep your spiritual fervor, serving the Lord."

## Discussion Questions
- Why does salvation (being saved from punishment for sin) give joy?
- Do you feel joy about your salvation? Why or why not?

## Prayer Prompter
Thank you for the joy we're able to have through being saved. We're thankful that through Jesus you have made it possible for us to live forever. Keep us following you always.

# Who Seeks God?
**Psalm 53**

## Memory Verse
*God looks down from heaven on the sons of men to see if there are any who understand, any who seek God (Psalm 53:2).*

## Attention Grabber
Play a quick game of hide-and-seek with the kids (indoors or out-doors).

## Living It
To "seek" means to look for something. God isn't hard to find. He wants to be found. He wants to save us and bless us. What he said to the Israelites in Jeremiah 29:11-13 he also says to us: "'For I know the plans I have for you,' declares the Lord, 'plans to prosper you and not to harm you, plans to give you hope and a future. Then you will call upon me and come and pray to me, and I will listen to you. You will seek me and find me when you seek me with all your heart.'"

## Discussion Questions
◉ What are ways you can seek God?
◉ In what ways do you know God better than you did when you were younger?

## Prayer Prompter
Please help us to seek you more and understand you better.

# God Hears

## Memory Verse

*Evening, morning and noon I cry out in distress, and he hears my voice (Psalm 55:17).*

## Attention Grabber

Ask the kids if they can imitate the sound of a test of the Emergency Broadcasting System. Ask what signal captains of ships send out when their ships are in distress (S.O.S.). Explain that anytime we're in distress, God will hear us.

## Living It

Aren't you glad that God is available twenty-four hours a day and seven days a week? It's amazing that the most powerful being in the universe is willing to make time for us. We can go to him as many times a day as we want!

## Discussion Questions

◉ Besides mealtimes, when do you usually pray during the day?
◉ What are some situations in which you call out to God for help?

## Prayer Prompter

Thank you for being willing to listen to us whenever we call out to you. Please help us to come to you every day.

# Cast Your Cares
### Psalm 55:18-23

## Memory Verse
*Cast your cares on the Lord and he will sustain you; he will never let the righteous fall (Psalm 55:22).*

## Attention Grabber
Float an empty margarine tub in a pan of water. Have the kids write problems on paper, crumple the paper into wads or fold the paper up, and try to toss the papers into the margarine tub. Point out that the tub won't sink, even with all the papers in it.

## Living It
Sometimes we may not tell our friends all of our problems because we don't want to weigh them down or discourage them, or because we don't want them to look down on us. If we tell God our problems, does he feel that way? Not a bit! He has compassion for us, but our problems don't burden him. He is able to give us the strength we need, and he can solve our problems much better than we could by ourselves.

## Discussion Questions
- How is worrying bad for us? (It can affect our health. It steals our joy. And it can make us prideful, trying to handle things without God.)
- What is a recent example of when you have trusted God with a problem and he took care of it?

## Prayer Prompter
Thank you for wanting to take our worries and problems. Please help us to have faith that you will help us solve them better than we can on our own.

# When I'm Afraid
## Psalm 56:1-4

## Memory Verse
*When I am afraid, I will trust in you (Psalm 56:3).*

## Attention Grabber
Have each kid write the memory verse on an index card. The kids can write the first half of the verse in shaky letters as if their hands are trembling with fear and then write the second half of the verse with steady hands. Ask, "At what times are you most afraid?" Have each child place his card in a spot where he may see it during his most scary times (for example, on the side of his nightstand if he's usually afraid at night).

## Living It
When we're afraid, we need to remember that God is with us. We can trust him to help us. No matter what situations we face, Jesus has promised that he will be with us always (Matthew 28:20). In John 14:27, Jesus said, "Do not let your hearts be troubled and do not be afraid." We can trust that no matter what happens, God will work things whatever way is best for us (Romans 8:28).

## Discussion Questions
- What are some times when you feel afraid? What comforts you?
- How does trusting God take away our fears?

## Prayer Prompter
Whenever we start to feel afraid, please remind us to trust in you.

# God Sees My Tears
**Psalm 56:5-8**

## Memory Verse

*Record my lament; list my tears on your scroll—are they not in your record? (Psalm 56:8).*

## Attention Grabber

Show the family a small bottle filled with water. Ask, "Do you think all of the tears you've cried could fill this bottle?"

## Living It

God knows every detail about us, even how many tears we have cried. Jesus says in Matthew 10:30 that God knows how many hairs are on our heads, too. We need to let God comfort us when we are sad. We should remember that our tears are temporary. In fact, if we follow God, someday we won't cry anymore. Revelation 21:4 says that there won't be any crying in heaven.

## Discussion Questions

- Have you cried recently? Why?
- How does it feel to see someone that you love cry? Do you think God feels that way about you when you cry? Why or why not?

## Prayer Prompter

Thank you for caring about us when we cry, Lord. Your love is a great comfort to us when we are sad.

# In God We Trust
### Psalms 56:9–59:17

## Memory Verse
*In God I trust; I will not be afraid. What can man do to me? (Psalm 56:11).*

## Attention Grabber
Let the kids place thin paper over coins and scribble lightly on the paper with pencils to make the phrase "IN GOD WE TRUST" appear (on U.S. coins).

## Living It
Have you ever heard a kid say, "My dad is bigger than yours!"? Your Father in heaven is bigger than anyone or anything. He is sovereign. That means he has unlimited power over everything that takes place. You can trust him in every situation.

## Discussion Questions
- When has God taken something that seemed bad and turned it into something good for you (for example, moving to a new house)?
- How has trusting God helped you in a frightening situation?

## Prayer Prompter
Help us and our whole country to have more trust in you. Help us remember that you are sovereign.

# Cling to God
## Psalms 60–63

### Memory Verse

*My soul clings to you; your right hand upholds me (Psalm 63:8).*

### Attention Grabber

Beforehand, wash and dry at least two pieces of polyester clothing. Don't use any fabric softener. Show how the clothes cling together. Or show how two magnets cling together. Emphasize that God wants us to cling tightly to him.

### Living It

God doesn't want our relationship with him to be distant. He wants us to cling tightly to him. He wants us to rely on him to hold us up and give us strength.

### Discussion Questions

◎ How close is your relationship with God?
◎ What would help you to be closer to God?

### Prayer Prompter

We love you, God. Thank you for wanting us to cling to you and rely on you to keep us standing.

**Cling to God**

# Awesome!
## Psalms 64–66

## Memory Verse
*Come and see what God has done, how awesome his works in man's behalf! (Psalm 66:5).*

## Attention Grabber
Take turns reading things God has done that are listed in Psalm 66:6-10. Let everyone have a chance to read. Emphasize that God does great things for us every day.

## Living It
The world is not like a toy top that God started spinning and then left alone. He is very involved in what happens on earth and in each of our lives. When we have a relationship with God in which we talk with him every day, it is very obvious to us that he is involved in our lives.

## Discussion Questions
- What has God done for you today for which you can praise him?
- What are things God has done for our family in the past for which we can be grateful?

## Prayer Prompter
Thank you for all you have done in our lives in the past, for what you are doing now, and for all that you will do in the future.

# Shine on Us
## Psalm 67

### Memory Verse

*May God be gracious to us and bless us and make his face shine upon us (Psalm 67:1).*

### Attention Grabber

Have family members close their eyes while you shine a lamp on their faces so that they can feel the warmth of the light. Ask, "How is being in God's presence similar to having light shining on us?"

### Living It

We need God! We need his graciousness and his kindness. We need his blessings. We need the warmth of feeling close to him.

### Discussion Questions

- In heaven we will be able to see God face to face. What do you think that will be like?
- Do you feel as if God smiles when he looks at you? Why or why not?

### Prayer Prompter

We need you! Please continue to be gracious to us and to bless us with what we need. Help us to feel the warmth of knowing that you are smiling as you watch over us.

# A Father to All
## Psalm 68:1-18

## Memory Verse

*A father to the fatherless, a defender of widows, is God in his holy dwelling (Psalm 68:5).*

## Attention Grabber

Give each kid two As and two Bs (paper cutouts, alphabet blocks, alphabet macaroni, twisted chenille stems, or alphabet cereal). Have each person try to make a word. Then show the kids that the letters spell "Abba," which means "Daddy" in Aramaic, a language Jesus spoke.

## Living It

Even though all families do not have earthly fathers in their homes, all families can have the heavenly Father there! God is Daddy to all who believe in his Son. Ephesians 1:5 says we are adopted as God's children through Jesus Christ. Romans 8:14, 15 says that if you are led by the Spirit of God, you are children of God. And it is by that Spirit that we call God "Abba, Father." God wants us to know that he is our Father. God wants us to help children who don't have earthly fathers. James 1:27 says, "Religion that God our Father accepts as pure and faultless is this: to look after orphans and widows in their distress and to keep oneself from being polluted by the world."

## Discussion Questions

◉ How can a boy who doesn't have a father grow up to be a good father himself? (try to be like his heavenly Father)
◉ What needs do fatherless families have that God can fill?
◉ What can you do for people you know without fathers?

## Prayer Prompter

Please bless all of the families who do not have fathers and husbands in their homes. Please help us to understand that you are our Father who defends, protects, provides for, and helps us.

# God Bears Burdens

## Psalm 68:19-35

### Memory Verse

*Praise be to the Lord, to God our Savior, who daily bears our burdens (Psalm 68:19).*

### Attention Grabber

Do the following activity with each family member one at a time. Have each family member get on her hands and knees. Pile several books on her back, and have her try to crawl with this burden. After everyone has had a turn, explain that Jesus wants to carry our burdens every day. Put the books into a backpack.

### Living It

It's hard to walk with the Lord if we're letting our own burdens weigh us down. God wants to help us carry our burdens. He wants to lift them from us every day.

### Discussion Questions

◉ How can you let go of your problems and let God carry them?

◉ Why does it take faith to let God carry your burdens?

### Prayer Prompter

Thank you for being willing to lift our burdens off of us every day! Right now each of us will take turns saying aloud a burden that we need to give to you today.

# In Deep Water

## Memory Verse
*Save me, O God, for the waters have come up to my neck (Psalm 69:1).*

## Attention Grabber
Let each family member make a snowman by stacking three large marshmallows, one on top of the other, and connecting them by pushing a drinking straw, pretzel stick, or peppermint stick through them. They can draw faces on the top marshmallows with toothpicks dipped in food coloring. Have them place the snowmen in coffee mugs. Then fill the mugs with hot cocoa (Make sure it's not too hot!) up to the "necks" of the snowmen.

## Living It
Why do people call having serious problems being in "deep water" or in "hot water"? How would it feel to be in deep water if you didn't know how to swim? When we see problems coming, we can call on God right then. We don't have to wait until the problems make us feel like we are drowning. But even if we've waited until we are in serious trouble, God will still help us.

## Discussion Questions
- What kinds of problems could make you feel like you're in deep water? How could God rescue you from those?
- Have you ever read Shel Silverstein's poem, "I'm Being Eaten by a Boa Constrictor" (from *Where the Sidewalk Ends,* Harper and Row, 1974)? If so, how is that like sin?

## Prayer Prompter
Thank you for rescuing us from deep trouble many times, Lord. Please take care of the problems that are rising up around us right now.

# Praise Pleases God

**Psalms 69:30–70:5**

## Memory Verse

*I will praise God's name in song and glorify him with thanksgiving. This will please the Lord more than an ox (Psalm 69:30, 31).*

## Attention Grabber

Tell each family member something you admire about him. Emphasize that just as we love to be praised, God does, too. It makes him happy when we sing songs of praise to him. Sing a praise song together.

## Living It

In Bible times, people burned oxen on altars as sacrifices to please God. But praising God with song pleased him even more. Singing still pleases God. God loves to hear our praise even when the singing is by those of us who can't carry a tune very well!

## Discussion Questions

◉ Which praise song best expresses the feelings in your heart?
◉ Where and when do you sing praises to God?

## Prayer Prompter

You are worthy of all praise, God. We will praise you with songs to show how much we love you.

# My Confidence

**Psalm 71:1-13**

## Memory Verse

*For you have been my hope, O Sovereign Lord, my confidence since my youth (Psalm 71:5).*

## Attention Grabber

Ask the children if they have ever heard of a wallflower. Explain that a wallflower is someone who wants to fade into the wall covering. This person tries not to be noticed, usually because she doesn't have much confidence. If you have wallpaper in your home, hold a scrap of it in front of a matching wall. Emphasize that everyone feels self-conscious at times, but God can be our source of confidence.

## Living It

God gives us confidence that we are made righteous through faith in Jesus (Romans 3:22) and that no matter what others think of us, God adores us. "How great is the love the Father has lavished on us" (1 John 3:1). Spending time with God makes us feel loved and secure. Feeling confident of God's love for us makes us able to tell others about his love for them. You don't have to wait until you're an adult to have this kind of relationship with God. You can start right now!

## Discussion Questions

- In what situations have you lacked confidence?
- How could thinking about God's feelings for you have helped you in those situations?

## Prayer Prompter

Thanks for being our hope and confidence in every situation. We're thankful we can be confident that we can be with you in heaven because of the loving sacrifice of your Son.

# Tell All Day
## Psalm 71:14-24

## Memory Verse
*My mouth will tell of your righteousness, of your salvation all day long, though I know not its measure (Psalm 71:15).*

## Attention Grabber
Have each child practice explaining salvation, so he is able to tell nonbelievers about Jesus. If you need help, see page 270.

## Living It
Before Jesus went up to heaven, he gave the Great Commission. That is when he said, "Therefore go and make disciples of all nations, baptizing them in the name of the Father and of the Son and of the Holy Spirit" (Matthew 28:19). He wants us to tell the whole world about him. Even if we don't understand everything about God, we can still tell others about him. We don't have to have all the answers. We can just point people to the One who does!

## Discussion Questions
◎ Have you told anyone about Jesus? How did that person react?
◎ Can you think of someone who would be glad to find out that Jesus is the way to heaven?

## Prayer Prompter
Thank you for saving us. Please give us the courage, words, and opportunities to tell others how accepting Jesus makes them able to go to heaven.

# Pray for Leaders

## Memory Verse

*Endow the king with your justice, O God, the royal son with your righteousness (Psalm 72:1).*

## Attention Grabber

Beforehand, find out the names of local and national government leaders if you don't already know them. (You can look them up on the Internet or call your city hall.) Write the names of these leaders in lists on index cards. Cut a slit in the lid of a shoe box and let the kids pretend to vote by putting the index cards through the slit. Then have the kids turn their "ballots" into prayer lists by reading each name and praying for that person. Encourage the kids to pray for the leaders regularly.

## Living It

Adults in a democratic country get to vote for the people they want to lead them. These leaders make important decisions every day that affect others. Some of the leaders follow God, and some of them don't. It's important for us to pray for these people. They need to have God's justice—his sense of what is right and fair. They need to be right with God so they can have his wisdom.

## Discussion Questions

◎ How do you feel when you hear that government leaders have done something wrong? How can you pray for them at times like that?

◎ Why would the devil like to tempt our leaders to do what's wrong?

## Prayer Prompter

Please help our leaders to know you. Help them to accept Jesus and follow him. Give them the wisdom and courage to make the right decisions.

# Hold My Hand
**Psalm 73**

## Memory Verse
*Yet I am always with you; you hold me by my right hand (Psalm 73:23).*

## Attention Grabber
Have the kids wash their hands so they can make handprint cookies. Roll out sugar cookie dough (store-bought or homemade) and have each family member place her right hand on the dough. Trace around each family member's hand with a toothpick. Have them lift their hands and then cut out the handprints with a blunt knife. Follow baking directions in the recipe or on the package. (For Cake Mix Cookies recipe, see page 269.)

## Living It
It is important for little children to hold their parents' hands so their parents can keep them from walking into danger. God wants to protect us that way, too. He wants us to have a relationship with him that is so close that we feel almost as if he is holding our hands and keeping us from walking off the path in the wrong direction. Holding the hand of someone we love gives us comfort and makes us feel safe. God wants to give us those feelings, too. He wants us to trust that we are in his hands.

## Discussion Questions
- What could have happened if your parents didn't hold your hand when you were a toddler?
- When has it given you comfort to hold your parent's hand?

## Prayer Prompter
Thank you for wanting us to feel as if you are holding our hands. Please help us to trust you to show us which way to go, and help us to feel the comfort you offer us.

# Day and Night

**Psalms 74–76**

## Memory Verse
*The day is yours, and yours also the night; you established the sun and moon (Psalm 74:16).*

## Attention Grabber
Let the kids make sun-shaped air fresheners for the car. First, have each of them draw a sun shape on a piece of yellow felt and cut out the shape. Next, have them write "The day is yours" on their sun shapes with a fine-point permanent marker. When they are finished writing, poke a small hole in the top of each sun shape. Have each child thread a loop of embroidery floss or curling ribbon through the hole and tie the ends in a knot. Have them spray air freshener or apply a few drops of potpourri essential oil on their sun shapes. If they have made more than you need, let the kids give the air fresheners as gifts.

## Living It
It is easier to give God our lives on a daily basis when we think about the fact that he is the one who actually made the days and nights. He is also the one who gave us life. Our time on earth is a gift from God that we need to use to serve him.

## Discussion Questions
◉ What is a way you can serve God in the daytime?
◉ How can you serve him in the evening?

## Prayer Prompter
Thank you for making day and night. We realize that our days and nights are a gift from you. Please help us use them to serve you by serving others.

# Remember!
## Psalms 77–80

### Memory Verse

*I will remember the deeds of the Lord; yes, I will remember your miracles of long ago (Psalm 77:11).*

### Attention Grabber

Tie a string or ribbon loosely around each child's right index finger. Explain that sometimes people tie strings around their fingers to help them remember things.

### Living It

Can you remember things well? God wants us to remember the things he has done for us and for Bible people. Remembering what he has already done builds our faith that he will help us, just as he has helped others. When David needed the courage to fight Goliath, he remembered what God had already done. David said, "The Lord who delivered me from the paw of the lion and the paw of the bear will deliver me from the hand of this Philistine" (1 Samuel 17:37).

### Discussion Questions

◉ What are some of the miracles in the Bible that you remember God did?

◉ What are some things you remember that God did for your family or friends?

### Prayer Prompter

Thank you for always being faithful to help us. Please bless us with the ability to remember all you've done, and build our faith that you will help us in the future, too.

**Remember!**

# Near God
## Psalms 81–84

## Memory Verse

*Better is one day in your courts than a thousand elsewhere; I would rather be a doorkeeper in the house of my God than dwell in the tents of the wicked (Psalm 84:10).*

## Attention Grabber

Have a family member pretend to be a doorkeeper. Have that person stand in the doorway and welcome everyone to the devotion.

## Living It

It doesn't matter what job God gives us to do for him. We will have more lasting joy doing anything for him than any temporary pleasure we would have from doing something wrong. It is difficult even to imagine how great it will be to live with God. First Corinthians 2:9 says, "No eye has seen, no ear has heard, no mind has conceived what God has prepared for those who love him."

## Discussion Questions

◉ What do you look forward to the most about heaven?
◉ What talents, abilities, and spiritual gifts has God given you? How could you use those to serve him? (See 1 Peter 4:10.)

## Prayer Prompter

We love you so much that we long to worship you in heaven. That is what we want more than anything. Help us to use our talents and abilities for you while we are here on earth.

# Abounding in Love
**Psalms 85:1–86:7**

## Memory Verse
*You are forgiving and good, O Lord, abounding in love to all who call to you (Psalm 86:5).*

## Attention Grabber
Give each person a plate. Let them take turns using dishwashing liquid to write the word "sin" on their plates. Then have them wipe the words out with their hands. Let the children rinse the plates and their hands with water. Emphasize that God forgives our sins and washes them away.

## Living It
Some people avoid God because they think he is up in heaven waiting to throw lightning bolts at people. God isn't that way at all! He loves everyone, and he forgives anyone who repents.

## Discussion Questions
◉ As you get to know God better through Bible study and prayer, do you find him to be different than you once thought? How so?
◉ How does it feel to know that you can have your guilt and shame about sin washed away? Fill in the blank: Being forgiven is like _____.

## Prayer Prompter
When we call out to you, we are amazed by how forgiving, good, and loving you are. Thank you for taking our sins away, being so kind to us, and caring so much about us.

# Walk in Truth
## Psalms 86:8–87:7

## Memory Verse

*Teach me your way, O Lord, and I will walk in your truth; give me an undivided heart, that I may fear your name (Psalm 86:11).*

## Attention Grabber

Use a plank of wood as a balance beam. Place the plank on top of three large cans so that it is raised several inches off the ground. Have two people hold onto the plank—one on each end. Let family members take turns trying to walk across it. Can everyone make it across? What about on one foot, backward, or on tiptoe?

## Living It

What does it mean to walk in God's truth? (to live his teachings) No one can walk in the truth perfectly all of the time, but God wants us to have willing hearts. The more we ask God to teach us his way, the more he will reveal that way to us. Having an undivided heart means that your whole heart is committed to God. Jesus said the most important command is to love the Lord your God (Mark 12:28-30).

## Discussion Questions

◎ What makes it difficult to walk in God's truth?
◎ What helps us to walk in God's truth?

## Prayer Prompter

We love you, Lord, and we give you our whole hearts. Please teach us and help us to walk in your truth.

# Firm Forever
## Psalms 88:1–89:8

### Memory Verse

*I will declare that your love stands firm forever, that you established your faithfulness in heaven itself (Psalm 89:2).*

### Attention Grabber

Show the kids a flagpole, deck post, or other object that is embedded in cement. Let them try to budge the object so they can see how firm it is. Emphasize that God's love for them stands even more firmly. Nothing can knock it down.

### Living It

There is nothing you can do that will ever stop God from loving you. He will always be faithful to listen to you, care about you, and help you. Romans 8:38, 39 says, "For I am convinced that neither death nor life, neither angels nor demons, neither the present nor the future, nor any powers, neither height nor depth, nor anything else in all creation, will be able to separate us from the love of God that is in Christ Jesus our Lord."

### Discussion Questions

- How would your personality be different if you didn't know that God loved you?
- What are ways God shows you that his love for you is firm?

### Prayer Prompter

Thank you for loving us all of the time, no matter what.

# God's Power
**Psalms 89:9-52**

## Memory Verse
*You rule over the surging sea; when its waves mount up, you still them (Psalm 89:9).*

## Attention Grabber
Make blue gelatin before the devotion time. When it is partially set, add gummy fish for fun, if you have them. Allow time for the gelatin to set completely. At devotion time, let the kids spread nondairy whipped topping on the gelatin to make choppy white waves. Then they can smooth out the waves to show how the sea might have looked when Jesus calmed it.

## Living It
Mark 4:35-41 tells the story about Jesus calming the storm. While the disciples were afraid of the storm, Jesus was calm. He had the power to make the wind and waves be still. Jesus has enough power to bring peace to any situation. We will never have a problem that is too big for him.

## Discussion Questions
◎ Would you have been afraid if you were on the boat with Jesus in the storm? Why or why not?
◎ In what ways do you need God's power in your life?

## Prayer Prompter
We praise how powerful you are, God. It makes us feel secure to know that no problems are too large for you.

# Wake to God's Love
## Psalm 90

### Memory Verse

*Satisfy us in the morning with your unfailing love, that we may sing for joy and be glad all our days (Psalm 90:14).*

### Attention Grabber

Print the letters P-R-A-Y with a computer or by hand for each child. Have the kids cut out the letters, color them, and tape them to their alarm clocks or beside their beds.

### Living It

There's a coffee commercial that says the best part of waking up is that brand of coffee in your cup. Actually, the best part of waking up is spending time with God and feeling his love. Try not to rush through your prayers; give yourself time to listen to the Lord and feel the love that he has for you. That will get your morning off to a great start and set the tone for the whole day.

### Discussion Questions

- What differences do you notice between days you start with prayer and days you don't?
- What can help you remember to pray in the morning?

### Prayer Prompter

Thank you for getting our days off to a good start by helping us feel your love for us when we pray. Help us remember to pray every morning.

# Angels to Guard You

## Memory Verse

*For he will command his angels concerning you to guard you in all your ways (Psalm 91:11).*

## Attention Grabber

For each child, cut a simple angel shape out of a potato or sponge. Have the kids press the angel stamps on an ink pad or in a saucer of paint and then press the stamps on large sheets of paper that can be used as gift wrap. Have them use markers to write the verse around the angels.

## Living It

Do you feel like angels are watching over you? Hebrews 13:2 says that some people have entertained angels without knowing it! Angels are servants of God (Hebrews 1:14). We can praise God for sending them to guard our ways, but we should not worship angels themselves (Colossians 2:18; Revelation 22:8, 9).

## Discussion Questions

- ◉ Who can tell the story of the talking donkey and the angel? (Numbers 22:21-38) How did that angel guard Balaam's way?
- ◉ What mistake did an angel keep Joseph the carpenter from making? (Matthew 1:18-21)

## Prayer Prompter

Thank you for loving us enough to command angels to guard our ways.

# Because We Love Him

**Psalm 91:14-16**

## Memory Verse

*"Because he loves me," says the Lord, "I will rescue him; I will protect him, for he acknowledges my name" (Psalm 91:14).*

## Attention Grabber

Cut refrigerated biscuits (from a can) into quarters and form the quarters into heart shapes. Fry the hearts in a buttered pan. Then let the kids shake each heart in a lunch sack containing a cup of confectioners' sugar. Emphasize that hearts are a symbol of love. Express your love for the Lord. Tell them that because you love God, you know you can trust him to protect and rescue you. Or show them emergency phone numbers of family and friends. Tell the kids that you know these people would rescue you if you were in trouble. Explain that you know God will be there for you in any emergency, too.

## Living It

If your loved ones were in danger, you would rush to help them. God feels the same way about his loved ones. Those who love God can trust him to rescue them and protect them.

## Discussion Questions

◉ Can you think of a physically harmful situation from which God rescued you? What was it and how were you rescued?
◉ What was a spiritually harmful situation from which God rescued you?

## Prayer Prompter

Thank you for protecting us, Lord, and for rescuing us from harmful situations. We love you!

# Make Music
## Psalms 92, 93

### Memory Verse
*It is good to praise the Lord and make music to your name, O Most High (Psalm 92:1).*

### Attention Grabber
Encourage everyone to sing a praise song or play one on an instrument. See page 263 for instruments the kids can make.

### Living It
What are some instruments you have wanted to learn to play? One of the great benefits of learning how to play an instrument is that you can use that instrument to worship God. Even when you are alone while singing or playing an instrument, you have an audience. God is listening!

### Discussion Questions
⊚ What is the difference between merely singing or playing a song and worshiping God with a song?
⊚ Has anyone ever dedicated a song on the radio to you? How would that be similar to the feeling God might have when we sing or play music to glorify him?

### Prayer Prompter
We love you, Lord. We want to show it by worshiping you with music. We hope our praise is pleasing to you.

# God Hears and Sees

## Memory Verse

*Does he who implanted the ear not hear? Does he who formed the eye not see? (Psalm 94:9).*

## Attention Grabber

Have the kids compare their ears and eyes. Which family members have ears that are shaped the same? Which have eyes that are the same color? Emphasize that God made everyone's ears and eyes.

## Living It

Your own face can remind you that God exists and that he hears and sees what takes place in the world. He gave you senses that he himself has. Psalm 94 says that God sees what everyone is doing and will eventually punish the wicked. Some people in the Bible thought God wasn't watching them. At King Belshazzar's party, people drank from the temple cups and praised false gods. Then a hand wrote on the wall. In Daniel 5:26-28, Daniel told the king the inscription meant "'*Mene:* God has numbered the days of your reign and brought it to an end. *Tekel:* You have been weighed on the scales and found wanting. *Peres:* Your kingdom is divided and given to the Medes and Persians.'" God knows what we are doing. He will reward each of us according to our actions (Psalm 62:12; Proverbs 24:12).

## Discussion Questions

◉ Have you ever wished that God couldn't see and hear you? If so, why?

◉ How does it help you to resist sin when you think about God watching and listening?

## Prayer Prompter

Thank you for our eyes and ears. Please help us to resist sin by remembering that you are watching.

**God Hears and Sees**

# Worship With Gladness

**Psalms 98:1–100:3**

## Memory Verse

*Worship the Lord with gladness; come before him with joyful songs (Psalm 100:2).*

## Attention Grabber

Play some praise and worship music. Encourage the kids to close their eyes and sing directly to God.

## Living It

Sometimes when it is time to worship in church, we do not feel glad and joyful. Sometimes we worry about what other people will think if they see us earnestly worshiping God. But that worry comes from pride. What matters is what God thinks. Our worship pleases him when it is sincerely from our hearts. If we sing to God when we have recently done something wrong, we might feel like hypocrites. At times like that, we need to tell God we're sorry and ask him for help to do better. Then his forgiveness will make us feel like singing.

## Discussion Questions

◎ Do you ever sing praise songs when you aren't in church? Why or why not?

◎ Why do you feel glad and joyful when you are worshiping God?

## Prayer Prompter

Thank you for giving us music as a way to worship you. Thanks for wanting us to feel joy and gladness.

# With Thanksgiving
**Psalms 100:4–101:8**

## Memory Verse
*Enter his gates with thanksgiving and his courts with praise; give thanks to him and praise his name (Psalm 100:4).*

## Attention Grabber
To get everyone feeling thankful, have everyone make fingerprint pictures of blessings. Have each child press his finger or fingers onto an ink pad and make at least ten fingerprints. The kids could make pictures representing the blessing of food by using their prints to make bunches of grapes. Or they could make people by drawing arms, legs, smiles, and other features on their prints. They could make fingerprint pets or cars or houses. Encourage them to be creative.

## Living It
When we come into God's presence as we're praying or worshiping, we should remember what he has done for us. We need to praise him for what he has already given us before we ask him for more. We can even be thankful for the privilege of entering God's presence. We're able to do that because of Jesus' sacrifice.

## Discussion Questions
- ⊙ Can you think of some blessing for which you've never thanked God? What is it?
- ⊙ How do you feel when you think about all that God has done for you?

## Prayer Prompter
We praise you for how generous and loving you are, dear God. Thank you for our many blessings.

**With Thanksgiving**

# His Benefits
## Psalms 102:1–103:5

### Memory Verse

*Praise the Lord, O my soul, and forget not all his benefits*
*(Psalm 103:2).*

### Attention Grabber

Let the kids paint the memory verse on their bedroom windows with water-based poster paints. Protect the floor and windowsill with newspaper. (Tip: Mixing paint with dishwashing liquid helps it stick to windows better and wash off more easily.)

### Living It

It's a privilege for us to know God. Let's take turns reading some of his benefits that are listed in Psalm 103:3-19.

### Discussion Questions

◉ What are the benefits of accepting Jesus as your Savior when you're young rather than later in life?
◉ What would your life be like if you had never heard about God?

### Prayer Prompter

Thank you for the many ways you show your love to us. We are thankful for the privilege we have of getting to know you.

# Far as East From West
## Psalms 103:6–106:48

### Memory Verse
As far as the east is from the west, so far has he removed our transgressions from us (Psalm 103:12).

### Attention Grabber
Go outside and have the kids look as far as they can east and west. Guess how many miles they might be able to see. Have them look through binoculars and a telescope, if those are available. Explain that east and west go on far beyond what we can see even with a telescope. If you have Morgan Cryar's song "What Sin?" from his *Love Over Gold* album, this would be a good time to play it.

### Living It
When we repent, it's like having Jesus throw our transgressions (our sins) so far away that they will never come near us again. The devil would like us to see sin more like a boomerang that keeps coming back. Another name for the devil is "the accuser." The devil tries to remind us of what we have done wrong, even when we have already repented. He gives us false guilt to discourage us so we feel unworthy to serve God. If we have been sincerely sorry for our sins and have trusted Jesus to take them away because of his sacrifice on the cross, we can trust that our sins are gone and we never have any reason to feel guilty about them again.

### Discussion Questions
- How does it make you feel to know that when you repent, God takes your sins away from you?
- What can you do to keep from repeating the same sin?

### Prayer Prompter
Thank you for taking our sins away. We are grateful that we can be clean because of Jesus. Please help us to forgive ourselves as you have forgiven us.

**Far as East From West**

# Don't Fear Bad News

## Memory Verse

*He will have no fear of bad news; his heart is steadfast, trusting in the Lord (Psalm 112:7).*

## Attention Grabber

Give family members sheets of newspaper. Have them write the verse across the columns with markers.

## Living It

All of us have bad news from time to time, but we don't have to be afraid. We can trust that even when bad things happen, God is sovereign. That means he is in control. When he doesn't get us out of what seems like a bad situation as fast as we would like, it may be because that situation is helping us grow (1 Peter 1:6, 7). If we look back at news that once seemed bad, we may be able to see how it actually turned out to be a blessing. Romans 8:28 says, "And we know that in all things God works for the good of those who love him, who have been called according to his purpose."

## Discussion Questions

◉ When have you received bad news and not been afraid? Why weren't you afraid?

◉ If your worst fear came true, what do you think would happen? How do you picture God helping you then?

## Prayer Prompter

Thank you for being so trustworthy. Help us remember that you are in control, so we don't need to worry even when we receive bad news.

# God Delivers
**Psalms 113–116**

## Memory Verse

*For you, O Lord, have delivered my soul from death, my eyes from tears, my feet from stumbling (Psalm 116:8).*

## Attention Grabber

Tie someone's shoelaces together and ask, "Why is this a bad idea?" (It may cause that person to stumble.) When the kids have had time to answer, ask them, "How is sinning like stumbling?"

## Living It

If we saw our shoelaces were tied together, we would untie them. As we're walking, if we see a hole or object in our path, we can avoid it. When we can see what might trip us up, we can avoid stumbling. God gives us commandments to keep us from stumbling into sin. Through his grace and the sacrifice of Jesus, we can be delivered from death and have life that lasts forever. God will take away the sadness of our sins and give us the joy of heaven (Revelation 21:3, 4). God does great things for us!

## Discussion Questions

◉ Why is Jesus called the Deliverer?
◉ How does God help you not to stumble?

## Prayer Prompter

Thank you for wanting to save us, forgive us, and help us stay away from sin.

# Run to God
**Psalms 117:1–118:9**

## Memory Verse

*It is better to take refuge in the Lord than to trust in man (Psalm 118:8).*

## Attention Grabber

Place the phone in front of everyone. Ask, "If we had an autodial button for God on our phone, would you call him every day?" Emphasize that getting in touch with God is even easier than that.

## Living It

When something good or bad happens to you, you may think of running to the phone to tell a friend. But we don't even need the phone to talk to the best friend of all! God is even more reliable than our friends. You'll never get his answering machine!

## Discussion Questions

◎ What do you trust other people to do for you?
◎ What are some reasons why trusting God is safer than trusting people?

## Prayer Prompter

Thank you for being worthy of our trust. We appreciate that you are always there for us.

# The Capstone
**Psalm 118:10-23**

## Memory Verse

*The stone the builders rejected has become the capstone (Psalm 118:22).*

## Attention Grabber

Open the box of a board game and ask the kids, "If I were cleaning and accidentally threw away some of the pieces of this game, which pieces could you do without and which ones are essential?"

## Living It

The capstone is a very important part of a building. If a builder threw away a capstone, he would regret it later when he saw how much he needed it. Jesus is the most important part of the church. Some people didn't realize that. They rejected Jesus and crucified him. But someday everyone will realize that Jesus is Lord (Philippians 2:10, 11).

## Discussion Questions

- In what ways do people still reject Jesus?
- In what ways does Jesus lead the church?
- What are ways to include Jesus in your life?

## Prayer Prompter

We are thankful to know that Jesus is Lord. Help us never to reject him.

# Rejoice and Be Glad
## Psalm 118:24-29

### Memory Verse
*This is the day the Lord has made; let us rejoice and be glad in it (Psalm 118:24).*

### Attention Grabber
If you know it, sing the song that is based on this verse. Have the kids tell something they are rejoicing about or are glad about today. If you would like, let them make stickers by writing the verse on blank mailing labels and decorating them.

### Living It
We don't have complete control over what happens to us from day to day, but we always have a choice about how to react. Sometimes the difference between good days and bad days is just the way we look at them. When we think about today being something God made, it helps us remember that he is in control of it and that he has good things in it for us. He will even use the difficult experiences to help us. Every day we have reasons to rejoice and be glad.

### Discussion Questions
◉ When you don't feel like rejoicing and being glad, what can you do to help yourself feel that way?
◉ How can other people tell when you're rejoicing and glad?

### Prayer Prompter
Help us to appreciate every day that you give us. Thank you for giving us reasons to rejoice and be glad.

# Hidden in My Heart

**Psalm 119:1-16**

### Memory Verse

*I have hidden your word in my heart that I might not sin against you (Psalm 119:11).*

### Attention Grabber

Beforehand, purchase a bag of colored rubber bands. During the devotion, ask the kids to recite to you every verse they have hidden in their hearts. Give each child a rubber band for each verse he remembers. The rubber bands can be wrapped around each other to form balls that will actually bounce.

### Living It

In the parable of the sower, the seed that was planted in good soil grew up and produced fruit (Matthew 13:23). What are the fruit of the Spirit listed in Galatians 5:22, 23? (love, joy, peace, patience, kindness, goodness, faithfulness, gentleness, and self-control) If we take God's Word to heart and try to apply it, the Holy Spirit will bring out good things in us and keep us from sinning.

### Discussion Questions

- When the devil tempted Jesus, how did Jesus respond (Matthew 4:1-11)? (He quoted Bible verses.)
- In the armor of God listed in Ephesians 6:14-17, which part is the Word of God? (sword of the spirit) How can you use that piece of armor?

### Prayer Prompter

Thank you for your Word. Please help us to take it to heart. Help us apply what we read to our own lives and remember what you've said so that we can fight temptations when they come.

# My Counselors
**Psalm 119:17-32**

## Memory Verse
*Your statutes are my delight; they are my counselors (Psalm 119:24).*

## Attention Grabber
Ask the kids to name their school counselors and to describe that job. Emphasize that a counselor usually helps a person figure out what steps to take to solve problems.

## Living It
People with serious problems often get counsel from the wrong places—from friends who aren't following Jesus, or even from talk shows. The best place to get counsel is from the Bible. God's statutes are his laws and guidelines for our lives. God gives them to us to help us know how to live lives in which we're doing what he wants and what is best for us. It's important to read the Bible daily even when we don't have specific problems, because what we learn will help us know what to do when problems come.

## Discussion Questions
- How can a concordance help you find the Bible's answers to your problems?
- How could reading the Bible accounts of each of these people help you know what to do in your own life: Abraham? (Trust God to keep his promises.) Moses? (Do what God has called you to do even when you're not confident.) Daniel? (Stand up for what's right.) Jonah? (Obey God when he first asks.)

## Prayer Prompter
Thank you for giving us counselors we can trust. We are grateful that your Word gives us answers about how to live.

# What's Worthwhile?
## Psalm 119:33-56

### Memory Verse
*Turn my eyes away from worthless things (Psalm 119:37).*

### Attention Grabber
Ask the kids if they ever feel like TV commercials waste their time. Emphasize that sometimes the TV shows do, too. Look through a TV program schedule together. Ask, "Are there any shows we've watched that were worthless, that didn't help us learn anything or even feel entertained?"

### Living It
If I swept the floor, the dustpan might have a couple coins in it or a piece of jewelry in it, but it would mostly have worthless dust and scraps of paper. I would keep what was valuable, but I would throw away what was useless. That's what we need to do with our lives. We need to keep what's good in our lives and get rid of what is worthless.

### Discussion Questions
- What are your favorite activities? Why do you like them?
- What are activities in your family's life that keep your family busy without adding any benefit? (You may want to look at the calendar while asking this.)

### Prayer Prompter
Please help us to know what activities waste our time and what activities matter. Keep us from giving our attention to things that aren't of any benefit, and especially guard us from things that cause us to sin.

# Give Understanding
## Psalm 119:57-80

### Memory Verse
*Your hands made me and formed me; give me understanding to learn your commands (Psalm 119:73).*

### Attention Grabber
Show the kids an instruction manual that came with an appliance, a toy, or software. Tell them something you wouldn't have known how to do without the manual.

### Living It
God's Word is like an instruction manual. It shows us how to live life the way God intended, full of faith and love. A lot of wisdom is packed into the Bible. Before we read it each day, it is wise to ask God to help us understand and learn.

### Discussion Questions
◉ What are some of God's commands that have helped you keep out of trouble?
◉ Why is it good to try to memorize God's Word?

### Prayer Prompter
Thank you for making us, Lord! Please help us to understand what the Bible says.

# A Lamp to My Feet

**Psalm 119:81-111**

---

### Memory Verse

*Your word is a lamp to my feet and a light for my path (Psalm 119:105).*

### Attention Grabber

Turn off the lights and have the family follow one person who is holding a flashlight. Ask what would happen if you turned off the flashlight or stopped looking at it. If you have Amy Grant's song "Thy Word" from her *Straight Ahead* album, this would be a good time to play it.

### Living It

A miner's hat is a hard hat with a light on it. If you were a miner, would you go into a dark mine shaft with your light off? We shouldn't go into the dark, sinful world without the lamp of God's Word lighting our path. We could lose our way without it. If we study the Bible and keep a close relationship with God, we don't have to be confused about what is right for us to do.

### Discussion Questions

◉ Have you ever sat reading in the dark until someone turned on the light for you? What change did it make? Why hadn't you turned on the light yourself? What prevents you from reading the Bible?

◉ Sometimes cartoons show a lightbulb going on over someone's head when she gets an idea. What have you read in the Bible that made a "lightbulb" go on for you?

### Prayer Prompter

Please light our path with your Word. Help us to be faithful about studying the Bible, and help us remember what we have read.

**A Lamp to My Feet**

# To the Very End
## Psalm 119:112-176

### Memory Verse

*My heart is set on keeping your decrees to the very end (Psalm 119:112).*

### Attention Grabber

Read half of the kids' favorite short story or poem. Stop abruptly in the middle of the story or poem. (Be ready for the kids to complain!)

### Living It

Are you someone who usually finishes what you start? Why or why not? It's important to set our hearts on following God throughout our lives. When we face temptations, we need to have our minds already made up not to give in to them. We need to rely on God to help us. First Corinthians 1:8 says, "He will keep you strong to the end, so that you will be blameless on the day of our Lord Jesus Christ."

### Discussion Questions

◉ What are some temptations you have already decided that you will resist?

◉ Picture yourself throughout your life. How do you see yourself serving God as a teen? as a married person? in your career or ministry? as an elderly person?

### Prayer Prompter

We love you, Lord, and we want to follow you always. Help us to stay true to you to the very end.

# My Help
## Psalms 120–123

### Memory Verse
*My help comes from the Lord, the Maker of heaven and earth (Psalm 121:2).*

### Attention Grabber
Beforehand, have each family member collect some twigs. Or give each of them brown chenille stems. Have the kids pretend they are stranded on a desert island and that they must use these "branches" to spell a message (such as "help" or "S.O.S.") for rescuers in airplanes and helicopters to see.

### Living It
Even though we're not shipwrecked, we need help every day. God is the one to go to for everything we need. We can ask him for help physically, emotionally, mentally, socially, and spiritually.

### Discussion Questions
- What are some situations in which you need help?
- What are ways God helps you directly? What are ways he helps you through other people?

### Prayer Prompter
Thank you for being our help in every situation we face!

# Unless God Builds It
## Psalms 124:1–127:2

### Memory Verse

*Unless the Lord builds the house, its builders labor in vain. Unless the Lord watches over the city, the watchmen stand guard in vain (Psalm 127:1).*

### Attention Grabber

Build a house of cards as shown on page 267. (If you don't have playing cards, you can use business cards or index cards.) Let the kids blow on the house and watch it fall.

### Living It

Sometimes we eagerly start projects without praying first. We need to make sure we are doing what God wants, and we need to ask him through prayer to direct our work. Otherwise, we might be wasting our time.

### Discussion Questions

- What is a project that you think may have failed because you didn't pray about it first? How do you think prayer might have helped you?
- Besides the Bible, what are ways God might let you know what he wants you to do?

### Prayer Prompter

Please help us to do the work that you want us to do.

# A Reward
## Psalms 127:3–129:8

### Memory Verse
*Sons are a heritage from the Lord, children a reward from him (Psalm 127:3).*

### Attention Grabber
Stick a gift bow on top of each child's head. Tell the kids that children are a gift from God.

### Living It
Taking care of children is hard work, but it's worth every minute of it. Children give their parents joy. Although children learn from their parents most of the time, parents can learn from kids, too. Jesus said that adults need to be humble like children (Matthew 18:4). Psalm 127:4, 5 compares children to arrows that can go out to defend their parents. Children can go into the world and help make the world a better place.

### Discussion Questions
◉ What can adults learn from children?
◉ How will you help your parents throughout your life?

### Prayer Prompter
Thank you for the gift of children, Lord. Help us always to treat them as gifts from you.

# God Forgives
## Psalms 130–132

### Memory Verse

*If you, O Lord, kept a record of sins, O Lord, who could stand? But with you there is forgiveness; therefore you are feared (Psalm 130:3, 4).*

### Attention Grabber

Have the kids write the memory verse on the sidewalk with paint-brushes dipped in water. As they watch the words evaporate, explain that when they ask God for forgiveness, their sins disappear.

### Living It

If someone loves another person, he forgives the person. He doesn't hold a grudge; he "keeps no record of wrongs" (1 Corinthians 13:5). God is love (1 John 4:8), so he "keeps no record of wrongs" when we repent. In 1 John 1:9, God promises that "If we confess our sins, he is faithful and just and will forgive us our sins and purify us from all unrighteousness."

### Discussion Questions

- ◉ Do you think God sees you as better or worse than you see yourself? Why?
- ◉ Do you have trouble forgetting sins for which you have already repented? Why or why not?

### Prayer Prompter

Thank you for forgiving us when we repent.

# A United Family
## Psalms 133–135

### Memory Verse

*How good and pleasant it is when brothers live together in unity! (Psalm 133:1).*

### Attention Grabber

Beforehand, photocopy a large photo of your family. Cut each family member's picture out as an individual puzzle piece. Or cut a piece of paper into a jigsaw puzzle with the same number of pieces as the number of people in your family. Write each person's name on a puzzle piece. Give each person her piece of the puzzle. Then let the whole family work to put the puzzle together.

### Living It

Each of us is an important part of our family. If we are all united (joined together), we feel good and our home is a pleasant place to be. If anyone in our family is not getting along well with anyone else, the whole family suffers. Even one person who is trying to be a peacemaker can make a big difference in the moods of everyone around her.

### Discussion Questions

◉ What is a happy memory you have of a time when your family all got along well and had a good time together?
◉ What are some things that you do when you are trying extra hard to get along with others?

### Prayer Prompter

Thank you for making us part of a family. Please help us to get along well with each other and stay close.

# God's Love Lasts
## Psalms 136, 137

### Memory Verse

*Give thanks to the God of heaven. His love endures forever (Psalm 136:26).*

### Attention Grabber

Give one of the kids a drum or an oatmeal container and have him do an impression of the Energizer® Bunny character. Explain that God's love is like that bunny—it keeps going and going. Or show them a wreath, and explain that it's a symbol of God's love, which never ends. Or draw the symbol for infinity (∞), and explain that the symbol, like God's love, doesn't stop.

### Living It

There is nothing that can separate us from the love of God (Romans 8:38, 39). His love is more reliable than anything else. Friends might not always stand by us and love us, but God always will. We can trust him. Do you remember the story about the lost son (Luke 15:11-24)? Even though he had done many wrong things, his father loved him anyway. When the runaway son came home, his father ran out to hug him! There is nothing we could ever do that would stop God from loving us.

### Discussion Questions

- What are some ways God has shown you that his love for you endures forever?
- How does knowing that God's love for you is eternal help you?

### Prayer Prompter

Thank you for loving us always.

# Search Me

**Psalms 138:1–139:6**

## Memory Verse

*O Lord, you have searched me and you know me (Psalm 139:1).*

## Attention Grabber

Beforehand, hide a toy or other object in the room. Have the kids search the room to find it.

## Living It

God searches our hearts. He can see everything that is in them. He even knows us better than we know ourselves, and he loves us in spite of our flaws. Let's read some of the things Psalm 139 says God knows about us.

## Discussion Questions

- Do you think your friends would like you if they knew everything about you? Why or why not?
- Why is it good that God knows everything about you?

## Prayer Prompter

Thank you for wanting to know everything about us and for loving us anyway!

# God Is Everywhere

**Psalm 139:7-12**

## Memory Verse

*If I go up to the heavens, you are there; if I make my bed in the depths, you are there (Psalm 139:8).*

## Attention Grabber

Give the kids "airplane rides" by swinging them around. (Make sure to hold the children under their armpits so you don't hurt their arms or shoulders.) Then let them "deep sea dive" by holding them upside down by their feet. Ask, "If you flew as high as airplanes could fly, would you be away from God? If you swam as deep in the ocean as a diver could go, would you be away from God?"

## Living It

If we spun the globe and pointed at cities, we would never find one where God wouldn't be with you. If we looked through a telescope, we could never find another place in the galaxy where God wouldn't be with you. Remembering that can help when we're tempted to sin. Also, when we are afraid or lonely, we can find comfort in knowing God is with us.

## Discussion Questions

- Have you ever tried to hide something from God? If so, how did you feel?
- When have you been especially glad that God was with you?

## Prayer Prompter

Thank you for always being with us.

# Before Birth
## Psalm 139:13

## Memory Verse

*For you created my inmost being; you knit me together in my mother's womb (Psalm 139:13).*

## Attention Grabber

Show the kids pictures of their mother when she was expecting them, ultrasound pictures of them before birth, or a photo of an unborn child that is tiny but fully formed. Mention that an unborn baby's heart begins beating in the fourth week of development and that some babies even suck their thumbs before they are born! (If your children are old enough, this may be a good time to explain to them what abortion is and why it is wrong.)

## Living It

God has known us since before we were even born. He told Jeremiah, "Before I formed you in the womb I knew you, before you were born I set you apart; I appointed you as a prophet to the nations" (Jeremiah 1:5). God knew us when he made us. Of course, he didn't actually use knitting needles and yarn to form us, but he did cause each of our cells to form. Every life is very important to him.

## Discussion Questions

◉ What about you was already set in place before you were even born? (eye color, hair color and type, some personality characteristics, general size, God's love for you, etc.)

◉ Which of your friends has known you the longest? (God has known you even longer than that!)

## Prayer Prompter

You've known us even longer than our family has! Thank you for creating us and for being with us our entire lives, even before our births.

# I'm Wonderfully Made
## Psalm 139:14-22

## Memory Verse

*I praise you because I am fearfully and wonderfully made; your works are wonderful, I know that full well (Psalm 139:14).*

## Attention Grabber

Let the kids sketch self-portraits. Or if you have time, let them make mannequins of themselves by stuffing newspaper into clothes they have recently outgrown. Either have them draw their faces on balloons and place hats on the balloon "heads," or have them tape cut-out, color copies of 8" x 10" close-ups of their faces to the balloons. Then attach the balloon heads to the tops of their stuffed shirts.

## Living It

When you look into a mirror, do you see a creation of God? You will treat yourself with more respect if you do. It's easier to like your eyes, nose, and other features when you remember that God made them. Try to see other people as being "wonderfully made," too.

## Discussion Questions

- Do you ever compare yourself to models and celebrities? Why or why not?
- How might someone who has respect for his own body act differently from someone who doesn't respect his body?
- Which of your body's senses do you value the most?

## Prayer Prompter

We're sorry for taking our bodies for granted and for complaining about them at times. Thank you for making us the wonderful way we are.

# Know My Thoughts
## Psalms 139:23–140:13

### Memory Verse

*Search me, O God, and know my heart; test me and know my anxious thoughts. See if there is any offensive way in me, and lead me in the way everlasting (Psalm 139:23, 24).*

### Attention Grabber

Place a bowl of popped popcorn, an empty bowl, and two cups on the table. Give the cups to two family members and have them race to see how many unpopped kernels they can remove from the popcorn and drop into their cups. (They can get the popped kernels out of their way by putting them into the empty bowl.) The player with the most unpopped kernels wins.

### Living It

It is generally good to remove or change things that are not working well or are causing problems. If you had serious pain in your body, you would want to go to a doctor and have him examine you to find out the cause of the pain. Then you would want that cause removed as quickly as possible. Sin causes pain and sorrow in our lives. We need to go to God and ask him to examine our lives and show us where we have sinned. We need to open our hearts and minds to God so he can get rid of anything that he finds offensive.

### Discussion Questions

- ◎ What are examples of "anxious thoughts"?
- ◎ When you pray, what things prevent you from opening your heart and mind to God?

### Prayer Prompter

Please remove everything offensive from our hearts and minds.

# Guard My Mouth
## Psalms 141–143

### Memory Verse

*Set a guard over my mouth, O Lord; keep watch over the door of my lips (Psalm 141:3).*

### Attention Grabber

Pretend to zip your lips together and then to unzip them. Ask the kids what it means to say, "My lips are sealed."

### Living It

It isn't easy to control what we say. James 3:8 says "no man can tame the tongue." We need God's help to control our tongues.
James 3:5 compares the tongue to a spark that sets a giant forest on fire. What we say can do a lot of damage! Our words can also do a lot of good. Ephesians 4:29 says, "Do not let any unwholesome talk come out of your mouths, but only what is helpful for building others up according to their needs, that it may benefit those who listen." James 1:19 says to be "quick to listen, slow to speak."

### Discussion Questions

- ◎ If you used bad language, what message would it give others about you?
- ◎ What can you say to others that encourages them?

### Prayer Prompter

Please help us to think before we speak. Please stop us from saying what we shouldn't. Help us to say only what will benefit others.

# Praise Every Day
## Psalms 144:1–145:2

### Memory Verse
*Every day I will praise you and extol your name for ever and ever (Psalm 145:2).*

### Attention Grabber
Beforehand, photocopy the "30 Days of Praise" chart from page 266 for each person. Or have everyone make a simple two-column chart, with one column for the date and one column for writing praises. Encourage everyone to write a different praise about God each day for the next four weeks or so. Play Ray Boltz's song "I Will Praise the Lord" from *The Altar* album, if you have it.

### Living It
What does extol mean? (lift up, praise highly, glorify) Some days we may not be in the mood to praise God. But when we talk about God's greatness, we will feel better. When Paul and Silas were beaten severely and thrown into prison, they probably felt more like crying than singing. But they sang praise to God anyway. Two miracles happened: an earthquake opened the prison gates, and the jailer and his family believed in God (Acts 16:22-34). What seemed like a horrible day turned out great after they praised God.

### Discussion Questions
◉ Can you make the same promise as the psalm writer? How can you plan to praise God every day for the rest of your life?
◉ Why is it easier to praise God on a good day than on a bad day? Why do we need to praise him on bad days, too?

### Prayer Prompter
We praise you for being with us always. Please help us remember to praise you every day.

# Slow to Anger
## Psalms 145:3–146:10

## Memory Verse

*The Lord is gracious and compassionate, slow to anger and rich in love (Psalm 145:8).*

## Attention Grabber

Beforehand, chill a bottle of molasses or honey. When it's time to have your devotion, get out the bottle and let one of the kids try to pour enough to fill a cup. Or have family members think of ways to finish the simile "as slow as _____." Explain that God is very slow to get angry.

## Living It

Don't ever worry that it's too late to tell God you're sorry. Some people think God is mean and mad at everyone. The opposite is true. He is kind to us even when we don't deserve it. He cares about our feelings and our circumstances. He is patient with us. He loves us very much.

## Discussion Questions

◉ Does it ever surprise you how loving God is to you even when you have done something wrong?

◉ Do you get angry easily or slowly? How can you be more like God in the way you handle your anger?

## Prayer Prompter

Thank you for loving us and being so patient with us. Help us to be slow to anger and rich in love as you are.

# Good to Sing Praises

**Psalms 147, 148**

## Memory Verse

*Praise the Lord. How good it is to sing praises to our God, how pleasant and fitting to praise him! (Psalm 147:1).*

## Attention Grabber

Have each family member sing the first line of her favorite praise song and tell how that song expresses her feelings for God.

## Living It

Let's take turns calling out all the verbs (action words) in Psalm 147 that refer to some of the great things God has done. There is no doubt that God deserves our praise. It is good to praise him because we owe him that praise. But it's also good to praise him because of how good it makes us feel.

## Discussion Questions

- Think of the verbs we mentioned. What has God done for you?
- What can you do today to praise God?

## Prayer Prompter

We give you our praise and our love. Thank you for blessing us in many, many ways.

**Good to Sing Praises**

# We Delight God
**Psalm 149**

## Memory Verse
*For the Lord takes delight in his people; he crowns the humble with salvation (Psalm 149:4).*

## Attention Grabber
Have the kids make crowns by tying together pieces of wrapped candy with pieces of string or ribbon.

## Living It
Did you know that you give God joy? He takes delight in you! He loves everyone in the world very much. He is happiest of all when we humble ourselves enough to admit that we need Jesus. Only through Jesus can we get to heaven. There is rejoicing in heaven when someone repents (Luke 15:7)!

## Discussion Questions
◉ Describe a time when your mom or dad "took delight" in watching you do something. Can you picture God looking at you that way? Why or why not?
◉ Why does a person need to be humble to accept salvation (being saved)? (We need to admit we sin and our good works can't get us to heaven. We have to realize that we need Jesus as our Savior.)

## Prayer Prompters
It makes us happy that you take delight in us! Help us to remain humbly aware of how much we need you.

# Ways to Praise
### Psalm 150

## Memory Verse
*Let everything that has breath praise the Lord. Praise the Lord (Psalm 150:6).*

## Attention Grabber
Have everyone take turns whistling a line from a praise song that the others can guess. Or if you have time, let the kids make instruments from page 263 to play while listening to a praise song.

## Living It
Our lives are full of reasons to praise God. The ability to breathe is designed by God, so it seems appropriate to use that breath to praise him! We can also praise him with the music of instruments, and in many other ways. We can praise him by praying, by talking about him to others, and by obeying his commands.

## Discussion Questions
◎ What other ways to praise God are listed in Psalm 150:3-5?
◎ What talents has God given you that you can use to praise him?

## Prayer Prompter
You are great, God! Thank you for giving us many reasons and many ways to praise you.

# Respect God

**Proverbs 1:1-7**

 ## Memory Verse

*The fear of the Lord is the beginning of knowledge, but fools despise wisdom and discipline (Proverbs 1:7).*

 ## Attention Grabber

Tell the kids you are going to try a new recipe. Start to look in the cookbook and then shut the book and say something like, "I'm tired of reading that dumb old book. I can make up that recipe all by myself." Then start gathering all sorts of odd ingredients as the kids protest. Ask the kids why it is good to follow directions.

 ## Living It

Proverbs 1 points out several differences between a wise person and a fool. Wise people have respect and reverence for God and want to learn from him. Fools don't even try to gain wisdom. When they are disciplined, they don't learn from it. When someone disciplines us, we shouldn't just get mad. Instead, we should try to understand how to improve the way we act.

 ## Discussion Questions

◎ What are ways you can show respect for the Lord?
◎ If you had never been disciplined when you did something wrong, how might you act today? What have you learned from being disciplined?

 ## Prayer Prompter

We respect you, Lord. Help us to gain wisdom and to learn when we are disciplined.

# Listen to Parents
## Proverbs 1:8, 9

 ### Memory Verse
*Listen, my son, to your father's instruction and do not forsake your mother's teaching (Proverbs 1:8).*

 ### Attention Grabber
Teach the kids to do something simple, such as make instant pudding, play "Chopsticks" on the piano, or draw.

 ### Living It
Parents teach their children because they love them and want them to have happy lives. Some things your parents teach you are just for fun, but other instruction may be important enough to save your life. The Bible says you need to listen and apply what your parents say. One of the Ten Commandments is about parents. What does it say? (Look up Exodus 20:12.)

 ### Discussion Questions
- Why might you live longer by obeying your parents?
- What are some skills you remember learning from your parents?
- What are some truths your parents have taught you?

 ### Prayer Prompter
Please help us to listen carefully to our parents and obey them.

# Don't Give in to Sin
## Proverbs 1:10-33

### Memory Verse
*My son, if sinners entice you, do not give in to them (Proverbs 1:10).*

### Attention Grabber
Put a pear half on a plate. Have one of the kids push down on the pear half with a potato masher. Say, "Don't give in to 'pear' pressure." When the kids groan and say, "You mean peer pressure," ask them to tell you what a peer is and how their peers try to pressure them.

### Living It
Sometimes other kids will try to tempt you to go against what the Bible says. It isn't always easy to do the right thing when others are doing wrong, but God will bless you for obeying him. God gave us commandments to save us from the sorrow and misery that sin causes. Just like the pear half was damaged, your life will be damaged if you follow sinners.

### Discussion Question
◎ What would your answers be if a peer asked you, "Why won't you shoplift?" or "Why won't you take illegal drugs?" or "Why don't you lie?" or "Why not gossip?"

### Prayer Prompter
We love you and want to obey you. Please help us to resist when people try to tempt us to do what's wrong.

# God Gives Wisdom
**Proverbs 2:1-11**

## Memory Verse
*For the Lord gives wisdom, and from his mouth come knowledge and understanding (Proverbs 2:6).*

## Attention Grabber
Make a large question mark on a table with string. Or, using a pineapple slice, form a question mark on a plate for each person. Cut each slice in half. Use one half of the slice as the curved part of the question mark. Cut the other half into pieces to form the straight part of the question mark and the period. Emphasize that all of us are full of questions. We need knowledge, understanding, and wisdom.

## Living It
God wants us to come to him for answers to our questions. We can gain wisdom, knowledge, and understanding by listening to God when we pray and read the Bible. It's tempting to get all of our advice from other people, but God is the best source.

## Discussion Questions
- Why is it important to go to God and study the Bible yourself instead of relying only on others to pray for you or tell you what is in the Bible?
- What has God shown you while you were reading your Bible or praying recently?

## Prayer Prompter
We praise you for your wisdom, knowledge, and understanding. Please remind us to pray and to read the Bible daily.

**God Gives Wisdom**

# Stay on the Path

**Proverbs 2:12-22**

## Memory Verse

*Wisdom will save you from the ways of wicked men, from men whose words are perverse, who leave the straight paths to walk in dark ways (Proverbs 2:12, 13).*

## Attention Grabber

On a tabletop, use toothpicks or string to make a straight and narrow path. Then make a wide and winding road that branches off that path. Turn a flashlight on and put it at the end of the straight path, with the light shining toward the path. Put a box or a can at the end of the winding path. As you push a toy car (or some other small item such as a matchbox) along the path, explain that some people are headed for a dead end, away from fellowship with God.

## Living It

Perverse means being turned away from what is right. It isn't wise to hang around perverse people because they can influence us to go down dark paths right along with them. "God is light; in him there is no darkness at all" (1 John 1:5); so if we walk in the dark, we are living without God's influence. First John 1:6 says, "If we claim to have fellowship with him yet walk in the darkness, we lie and do not live by the truth."

## Discussion Questions

- What is it like to be in the dark physically? What is it like to be in the dark spiritually?
- How do your friends influence you in both good and bad ways?

## Prayer Prompter

Please give us the wisdom to choose friends that will encourage us to stay in your light.

# Loving and Faithful

## Memory Verse

*Let love and faithfulness never leave you; bind them around your neck, write them on the tablet of your heart (Proverbs 3:3).*

## Attention Grabber

Spread strawberry cream cheese or peanut butter in a heart shape on a slice of bread for each child. Have the kids use toothpicks to write "love" and "faithfulness" in the hearts.

## Living It

Have you ever seen words carved in stone or written in cement? They're permanent! God wants love and faithfulness to become permanent parts of our character. Some people wear necklaces to remind them of someone or something special to them. God wants the qualities of love and faithfulness to be special to us. He wants love and faithfulness to be in our hearts permanently. What are the greatest commandments? (Love God and other people, Matthew 22:36-40.) We show love to God by being faithful in obeying him (John 14:15).

## Discussion Questions

◎ When you think of keeping God's commandments, do you think of love? Why or why not?
◎ What does it mean to be faithful to God?

## Prayer Prompter

Thank you for being loving and faithful, God. Please help us to become more like you in those ways.

# Trust in the Lord
## Proverbs 3:5, 6

### Memory Verse
*Trust in the Lord with all your heart and lean not on your own under-standing; in all your ways acknowledge him, and he will make your paths straight (Proverbs 3:5, 6).*

### Attention Grabber
Ask the kids to quote the "eenie, meenie, miney, mo" rhyme for decision making. Ask how they would feel if you were trying to choose a new house and you made the decision by saying that rhyme. Emphasize that we need God's help in our decision making.

### Living It
What does it mean to trust God with all your heart? It means to trust him with every part of your life, to believe in what he says without doubting. Instead of making your decisions all on your own, let God help you make them. He sees a much bigger picture than you see. Trust what he tells you to do, even if you don't understand why. Listen to him throughout the day, through his Word and prayer, and by paying atten-tion to your conscience. Stay on the straight path he sets before you.

### Discussion Questions
- ◉ What are some decisions you have trusted God to help you make lately?
- ◉ Why does God expect us to obey him even when we don't understand the reason?

### Prayer Prompter
Help us to trust you with our whole hearts. Remind us to let you help us make our decisions.

**Trust in the Lord**

# God's Discipline
**Proverbs 3:7-12**

## Memory Verse
*The Lord disciplines those he loves, as a father the son he delights in (Proverbs 3:12).*

## Attention Grabber
Ask the kids if they think your family's discipline techniques work. Ask them, "What kinds of discipline would you use if you had kids?"

## Living It
Sometimes parents say "This will hurt me more than it will hurt you" before punishing their kids. Parents don't enjoy disciplining their kids; but they discipline their kids because they love them. If your parents didn't care, they wouldn't discipline you. They want you to grow up knowing what is right. God disciplines us for the same reason. He lets us suffer the consequences of our actions so that we can learn from them. He lets us go through trials that will help us learn to be humble and to rely on him. No one likes to be punished, but discipline teaches us and helps us to become the way God wants us to be (Hebrews 12:11).

## Discussion Questions
◉ How do you know that your parents love you even while they're punishing you?
◉ How do you know that God loves you even when his discipline seems hard?

## Prayer Prompter
Thank you for loving us enough to discipline us. Help us to learn quickly from your discipline.

# The Value of Wisdom
## Proverbs 3:13-26

 ### Memory Verse

*Blessed is the man who finds wisdom, the man who gains understanding, for she is more profitable than silver and yields better returns than gold. She is more precious than rubies; nothing you desire can compare with her (Proverbs 3:13-15).*

 ### Attention Grabber

Show the kids objects in your house that have gold, silver, or a gemstone on them. Explain why these items are more valuable than others. Tell them that wisdom and understanding are more valuable than silver, gold, or rubies.

 ### Living It

Wisdom and understanding are definitely worth seeking. Ask God for them. Also, try to learn from the Bible and from the people and situations God puts into your life. Ask yourself often, "What is God trying to teach me through this?"

 ### Discussion Questions

- How would having wisdom help you in your relationships? in your schoolwork? in planning your life?
- Would you rather be very poor and wise or very rich and unwise? Why?

 ### Prayer Prompter

We praise you for your wisdom. Please help us to become wise, too.

# Give Now
## Proverbs 3:27-30

### Memory Verse

*Do not withhold good from those who deserve it, when it is in your power to act. Do not say to your neighbor, "Come back later; I'll give it tomorrow"—when you now have it with you (Proverbs 3:27, 28).*

### Attention Grabber

Fill a cup of sugar and place it on the table. Say, "Has a neighbor ever asked us for a cup of sugar or another favor? What did we do? What are other favors people might ask of us?"

### Living It

Whenever we are able to do something good for someone who needs our help, God wants us to do it right then. Often it won't be convenient to help others right when they ask, but God doesn't want us to be selfish or to procrastinate. Some people need help right when they ask for it. It is wrong to stall and hope that they will forget to ask again. The Golden Rule says that we should treat others as we would want to be treated (Luke 6:31).

### Discussion Questions

◉ Why would it be wrong to stall when asked to do something good?

◉ What does the Golden Rule say? (Luke 6:31) Why is it a good idea to follow the Golden Rule?

### Prayer Prompter

Please help us to serve people willingly when they need us.

**Give Now**

# Don't Be Violent
## Proverbs 3:31-35

## Memory Verse
*Do not envy a violent man or choose any of his ways (Proverbs 3:31).*

## Attention Grabber
Play violin music or ask the kids if they know someone who plays the violin. Ask, "Why do some people have bumper stickers that say, 'Stop the violins!'?" When the kids groan and say, "No, it's 'Stop the violence!'" ask them to explain what violence is. Or take them to a toy store (or look at a toy catalog) and have them point out which toys are violent. Ask, "Is being violent a sign of strength? Why or why not?"

## Living It
Violent people try to make others afraid of them. They want to force people to give them what they want. God says not to be jealous of people who are like that and not to become violent ourselves. Sometimes TV shows and movies make violence seem to be a good way to solve problems, but it's not. It is against the law for people to attack other people and hit them—against the government's laws and against God's laws. Ephesians 4:31, 32 says, "Get rid of all bitterness, rage and anger, brawling and slander, along with every form of malice. Be kind and compassionate to one another, forgiving each other, just as in Christ God forgave you."

## Discussion Questions
◉ What are some violent actions in TV shows and movies?
◉ How can you calm down when you feel angry enough to hit someone or break something?

## Prayer Prompter
Please help us to love people like you do so that we never want to harm anyone. Help us to look up to people who are good role models, not violent ones.

# Our Bright Path

**Proverbs 4:1-19**

## Memory Verse

*The path of the righteous is like the first gleam of dawn, shining ever brighter till the full light of day (Proverbs 4:18).*

## Attention Grabber

Wear sunglasses and tell the kids, "Our future looks so bright that I need my shades!" If you want, let the kids wear sunglasses during the devotion.

## Living It

The future is bright for believers. Jesus said he is the light of the world (John 8:12). As we seek him, he reveals himself to us more. Eventually we will see him in his glory (Matthew 25:31). As you follow the Lord, you will become more and more aware of how he wants to use your life to help others. Don't worry if you can't see his whole plan for you at once. Try to follow him every day, and your path will become more clear to you.

## Discussion Questions

- The Bible and Jesus are both called "the Word." Do you remember what Psalm 119:105 says? "Your word is a _____ to my feet and a _____ for my path."
- What do you look forward to about following God in the future?

## Prayer Prompter

Lord, we want to know you and your will for us. As we seek you throughout our lives, please make our paths more clear.

# Guard Your Heart
## Proverbs 4:20-23

### Memory Verse

*Above all else, guard your heart, for it is the wellspring of life (Proverbs 4:23).*

### Attention Grabber

Ask the kids if they have ever seen or heard of springs of water. As you pour everyone a glass of water (bottled spring water, if available), explain that before people had sinks and faucets, they had to get water from springs or wells in the ground. They tried to keep dead animals and other harmful things out of their wells or springs so the water would remain pure.

### Living It

God says that in the same way that people try to keep their water supply pure, we need to keep our hearts pure. We need to make sure the things we feel and want are right. The emotions and desires in our hearts will influence our actions.

### Discussion Questions

◎ What are some things that can pollute your heart?
◎ What are ways you can guard your heart?

### Prayer Prompter

Please purify our hearts from anything that has polluted them. Help us guard our hearts against evil.

# Pure Speech
## Proverbs 4:24-27

### Memory Verse
*Put away perversity from your mouth; keep corrupt talk far from your lips (Proverbs 4:24).*

### Attention Grabber
Tell a clean joke or read a few from a book of clean jokes. Ask the kids what they do when someone tells a dirty joke or says something else bad and then laughs about it.

### Living It
One of the first ways people can tell the difference between believers and nonbelievers is by what they say. It's hard to be the salt of the earth if our language is peppered with profanity! First Timothy 4:12 says young people should "set an example for the believers in speech." Colossians 3:8-10 says to rid yourself of filthy language because you are trying to be like God. First Peter 3:10 says, "Whoever would love life and see good days must keep his tongue from evil and his lips from deceitful speech."

### Discussion Questions
◉ What can you say if other kids tease you about not cussing or saying other inappropriate words?
◉ How is it possible to be deceitful even while "technically" telling the truth? while staying silent?

### Prayer Prompter
Please help us to say only what you will be glad to hear.

# Rejoice in Marriage

**Proverbs 5:1-20**

## Memory Verse
*May your fountain be blessed, and may you rejoice in the wife of your youth (Proverbs 5:18).*

## Attention Grabber
(Most children hear more immoral views about sex than their parents expect. Counter that by emphasizing the positive aspects of sex in marriage so they will understand God's plan for it to be joyful, not shameful.) Place pieces of white chocolate on a pretty plate. Explain that chocolate for breakfast would make most people feel sick, but if they ate it after dinner, they would enjoy it. If people have sex before marriage, it makes them feel spiritually sick and guilty. If they wait until after they are married, sex can be a very unifying and joyful part of marriage.

## Living It
God wants husbands and wives to be faithful and to show each other that they love each other. One of the ways they do this is by having sex. Outside of marriage, sex is wrong; but inside of marriage, sex is part of God's plan. He wants husbands and wives to be happy and united as "one flesh" with each other in this kind of relationship (Mark 10:7, 8). He wants them to stay attracted to each other and to resist temptations to commit adultery, which can break apart families.

## Discussion Questions
◉ Why shouldn't people have sex before they are married?
◉ Why does adultery usually ruin marriages?

## Prayer Prompter
Help us to stay pure, Lord. If we marry, please help us to have a happy, united marriage.

# Snares of Sin
**Proverbs 5:21-23**

## Memory Verse

*The evil deeds of a wicked man ensnare him; the cords of his sin hold him fast (Proverbs 5:22).*

## Attention Grabber

Have everyone search for a spider web. Or give the kids twine, scissors, glue, and paper so they can make webs on the paper.

## Living It

When we sin, the devil is like a spider wrapping cords around us. Sin can paralyze us and keep us from being able to serve God.

Before people are born again in Christ, they are slaves to sin (Romans 6:17, 18). But believers can break free of sin with God's help. First Corinthians 10:13 says, "God is faithful; he will not let you be tempted beyond what you can bear. But when you are tempted, he will also provide a way out so that you can stand up under it." In the Lord's Prayer, Jesus said we should pray "deliver us from the evil one" (Matthew 6:13).

## Discussion Questions

- Have you ever seen how one sin can lead to another? What are some examples?
- When you get tangled up in sin, how do you get out?

## Prayer Prompter

Please forgive us for our sins and keep us from being tangled up in more of them.

# Learn From the Ants
**Proverbs 6:1-8**

## Memory Verse
*Go to the ant, you sluggard; consider its ways and be wise!*
*(Proverbs 6:6).*

## Attention Grabber
Make "ants on a log" by filling celery sticks with peanut butter and topping them with raisins. If you have time, go outside to watch some ants. The kids can even make miniature snacks for the ants by rolling tiny scraps of bread between their fingers and winding them to look like tiny cinnamon buns. Emphasize what hard workers the ants are.

## Living It
We can learn a lot from uninvited picnic guests. Let's read Proverbs 6:6-8. These verses explain that ants are hard workers. God wants us to be hard workers, not lazy like sluggards. Colossians 3:23 says, "Whatever you do, work at it with all your heart, as working for the Lord, not for men." The verses in Proverbs 6 also mention that ants plan ahead. Saving for the future makes good sense.

## Discussion Questions
◉ Have you ever had a day in which you accomplished more than you expected? How did you feel?
◉ Why is it wise to save some of the money you earn?

## Prayer Prompter
Please help us to work hard and plan ahead like the ants.

# You Snooze, You Lose

**Proverbs 6:9-15**

## Memory Verse

*A little sleep, a little slumber, a little folding of the hands to rest—and poverty will come on you like a bandit and scarcity like an armed man (Proverbs 6:10, 11).*

## Attention Grabber

Carry a pillow. When the kids ask why you have a pillow, explain that you will keep it with you so you can doze off whenever you feel like it. Ask if they see any problems with doing that.

## Living It

Proverbs 20:13 says, "Do not love sleep or you will grow poor." This verse doesn't mean that we shouldn't get rest to keep our bodies healthy. Of course, God wants us to sleep! But God doesn't want us to waste our days. He wants us to make the most of the time that we have. He wants us to be responsible for the work that we have to do. It is good to rest when we need a break, but that doesn't mean we should just lounge around all day.

## Discussion Questions

◉ What work does each person in your family do?
◉ Are there parts of your day that you are wasting?

## Prayer Prompter

Please help us not to be lazy. Help us to find the best ways to use our time.

# What God Hates

## Memory Verse

*There are six things the Lord hates, seven that are detestable to him: haughty eyes, a lying tongue, hands that shed innocent blood, a heart that devises wicked schemes, feet that are quick to rush into evil, a false witness who pours out lies and a man who stirs up dissension among brothers (Proverbs 6:16-19).*

## Attention Grabber

Teach the kids motions for each part of this verse: put your nose up in the air, stick out your tongue, use your hands to pretend to choke a neck, pat out the beat of a heart on your chest, run in place, hold up your right hand with your first two fingers crossed (to show you are lying), and stir with an imaginary spoon. Have your family say the memory verse together using the motions.

## Living It

Hate is a very strong word, and God doesn't use it often. Since he hates what is mentioned in the memory verse, we need to be especially careful to avoid those behaviors. An easy way to do that is to focus on loving God and loving people. If we feel love for them, we will want to obey God and not treat people in bad ways like those listed in the memory verse.

## Discussion Question

◉ How can you use each part of the body mentioned in the memory verse for good instead of bad?

## Prayer Prompter

We want to please you, Lord. Help us to love you and other people more. Help us to get rid of attitudes and behaviors that you hate.

# Adultery Causes Pain
**Proverbs 6:20–7:27**

## Memory Verse

*Can a man scoop fire into his lap without his clothes being burned? Can a man walk on hot coals without his feet being scorched? So is he who sleeps with another man's wife; no one who touches her will* go unpunished *(Proverbs 6:27-29).*

## Attention Grabber

Show the kids charcoal briquettes. If you have time, light the charcoal and cook on the grill. Emphasize how dangerous the coals are when they are hot and how painful it would be to have them land in your lap or to walk on them.

## Living It

It's unpleasant to think about sin and to talk about it, but it's important for you to know what is right and wrong. Jesus said to be as "shrewd as snakes and as innocent as doves" (Matthew 10:16). We need to be aware of what is wrong so we don't do it. It is very wrong for a person to have sex with someone he has not married. The pain of adultery is like the pain of a bad burn. Both can cause damage deep inside a person and both have lasting effects. When anyone commits adultery, there are always serious, painful consequences.

## Discussion Questions

- Which of the Ten Commandments names the sin in the memory verse?
- What are some of the consequences for people who commit adultery?

## Prayer Prompter

Help us to make firm commitments to stay morally clean. And, if we marry, help us to be faithful to our spouses.

**Adultery Causes Pain**

## Memory Verse

*"Do not rebuke a mocker or he will hate you; rebuke a wise man and he will love you" (Proverbs 9:8).*

## Attention Grabber

Share with the kids an experience in which someone's criticism helped you to overcome a flaw and you were grateful the person had mentioned it.

## Living It

To rebuke someone means that you express strong disapproval of what someone has done wrong. There is no point in correcting someone who won't change and will only hate you for it. Titus 2:15 says to "encourage and rebuke with all authority. Do not let anyone despise you." What is a good way to rebuke someone? Second Timothy 4:2 says to rebuke "with great patience and careful instruction." If you need to rebuke someone, you should treat that person with respect and love, as if she were one of your family (1 Timothy 5:1, 2). We need to be very careful not to hurt people's feelings, and we need to try not to be hurt when people criticize us. Proverbs 9:8 also shows us that a wise person is grateful to be told when she has done something wrong so she may change and do right.

## Discussion Questions

- Have you ever wanted to rebuke someone? Why or why not?
- What is the difference between an insult and criticism?

## Prayer Prompter

Please help us to know when it's right to rebuke people and how to do it gently. Help us learn from the criticism of others and not let it hurt our feelings.

# Bring Joy to Parents
## Proverbs 10:1-3

 ### Memory Verse
*A wise son brings joy to his father, but a foolish son grief to his mother (Proverbs 10:1).*

 ### Attention Grabber
Compliment each child for a way he has shown wisdom. If it is convenient, show a visual example (such as a book report a child did on time, a baptismal certificate representing a wise decision, or a photo showing a friendship that was a wise choice).

 ### Living It
A fool is someone who makes unwise decisions. Parents love their children. So when a child gets hurt by a foolish choice, the parents feel bad, too. Parents also have to endure the consequences of their children's mistakes. When children make wise decisions, parents are happy because they can see their children benefit from good choices.

 ### Discussion Questions
- What is an example of a foolish behavior you plan to avoid and a wise action you plan to do?
- What might be the consequences of the foolish behavior and the benefits of the wise action you mentioned?

 ### Prayer Prompter
Help us to be wise and bring joy to our parents.

# Hard Work
## Proverbs 10:4, 5

## Memory Verse

*Lazy hands make a man poor, but diligent hands bring wealth (Proverbs 10:4).*

## Attention Grabber

Trace around everyone's right hand on construction paper. Have each child cut out her hand shape, write the memory verse on it, and tape it to a wall or window.

## Living It

Laziness wastes time that a person could be using to earn a living or to take care of other important things. Ecclesiastes 10:18 says, "If a man is lazy, the rafters sag; if his hands are idle, the house leaks." When Adam had to leave the garden of Eden, God said, "By the sweat of your brow you will eat your food" (Genesis 3:19). Second Thessalonians 3:11, 12 says, "We hear that some among you are idle. They are not busy; they are busybodies. Such people we command and urge in the Lord Jesus Christ to settle down and earn the bread they eat."

## Discussion Questions

◉ How will the work you do in school now prepare you to earn a living later?
◉ If you work diligently and God gives you wealth, how will you use it to help others?

## Prayer Prompter

Please help us not to be lazy, and to make ourselves work hard until our responsibilities are fulfilled.

# What's Left Behind

**Proverbs 10:6, 7**

---

## Memory Verse

*The memory of the righteous will be a blessing, but the name of the wicked will rot (Proverbs 10:7).*

## Attention Grabber

Using your church phone directory, read aloud names of people who have been a blessing to your family. Have each family member write a brief thank-you note to one of these people.

## Living It

Sometimes people sign yearbooks or autograph albums with the message, "2 sweet 2 be 4 gotten." Has anyone written that to you? People who follow God bless the lives of everyone around them, and those who know them remember the good they did long afterward.

## Discussion Questions

- What is the kindest thing anyone has ever done for you?
- How does it help your faith to be around believers who follow Jesus?

## Prayer Prompter

Thank you for the faithful people who have had a great influence on our lives. Help our lives to bless others, too.

# Nothing to Hide
**Proverbs 10:8, 9**

## Memory Verse
*The man of integrity walks securely, but he who takes crooked paths will be found out (Proverbs 10:9).*

## Attention Grabber
Wear a trench coat if you have one and ask what kinds of evidence detectives find at crime scenes. Let the kids record their fingerprints by pressing their index fingers on an ink pad and then on index cards.

## Living It
Someday everyone's secrets will be revealed. Luke 12:3 says, "What you have said in the dark will be heard in the daylight, and what you have whispered in the ear in the inner rooms will be proclaimed from the roofs." Someone with integrity faithfully stays on God's straight and narrow path. He doesn't have to worry when he is accused of doing something wrong. He can say, "I have nothing to hide!"

## Discussion Questions
◎ When you have done something wrong, have other people usually discovered it? How did you feel when your wrong action was revealed?

◎ How can covering up wrongdoing lead to even more sin?

## Prayer Prompter
Please help us to live with integrity so that we will not have anything to hide.

# Love Covers Wrongs

**Proverbs 10:10-12**

## Memory Verse

*Hatred stirs up dissension, but love covers over all wrongs (Proverbs 10:12).*

## Attention Grabber

Ask the kids what they do when they have a "bad hair day." Put on a hat and say that just as a hat helps people overlook imperfections in a hairstyle, love helps us overlook imperfections in people. Even though we may know their faults (Everyone has them!), love helps us to look past their flaws and accept them as they are.

## Living It

If you love someone, you don't complain about her faults all the time, fight over nitpicky issues, or hold a grudge against that person because she did something wrong. In 1 Corinthians 13:4-7, Paul tells us that love is patient, kind, and doesn't keep a record of wrongs. When you are trying to get along with others, even difficult people, try thinking about how to love them more and it will be easier to overlook their faults.

## Discussion Questions

◉ How does hate stir up fighting and disagreements?
◉ What can help you to love people more so that you're willing to overlook their flaws?

## Prayer Prompter

Please help us to love the people around us enough to overlook their flaws and to try to get along with them.

**Love Covers Wrongs**

# Show the Way

### Memory Verse
*He who heeds discipline shows the way to life, but whoever ignores correction leads others astray (Proverbs 10:17).*

### Attention Grabber
Play a silly variation of "Pin the Tail on the Donkey" (for example, "Tape the Nose on the Supermodel") using clippings from a magazine. Blindfold each child, spin him, and let him try to tape the part onto the picture.

### Living It
When you are blindfolded, you want someone to guide you and tell you if you are going the wrong way. You want to be pointed in the right direction. When your leaders and parents correct you, it's important to listen. If you're drifting off in the wrong direction, you could cause others to drift, too.

### Discussion Questions
- ◎ Who steers you?
- ◎ In what ways have other people followed what you've done?

### Prayer Prompter
Help us to be humble enough to listen when parents and leaders try to steer us in the right direction.

# Hold Your Tongue
**Proverbs 10:19-24**

## Memory Verse
*When words are many, sin is not absent, but he who holds his tongue is wise (Proverbs 10:19).*

## Attention Grabber
Have the kids literally hold their tongues while trying to recite the memory verse. If you have a box of tic®tac fresh mints, have each child try to shake just one mint out of the container. Emphasize that it's hard to keep our words from spilling out.

## Living It
It's important to think before you speak so you "do not let your mouth lead you into sin" (Ecclesiastes 5:6), such as gossip, bragging, or saying hurtful things. Ephesians 4:29 says, "Do not let any unwholesome talk come out of your mouths, but only what is helpful for building others up according to their needs, that it may benefit those who listen."

## Discussion Questions
◉ What are examples of things you say that are beneficial to others and things that aren't?
◉ Is it hard for you to be careful about what you say? Why or why not?

## Prayer Prompter
Please help us to be careful what we say.

# Stand Firm Forever
**Proverbs 10:25-32**

## Memory Verse
*When the storm has swept by, the wicked are gone, but the righteous stand firm forever (Proverbs 10:25).*

## Attention Grabber
Have kids practice making storm sound effects, such as running tap water, tapping on a cookie sheet, dropping dried beans in a cardboard box, and howling like the wind. Record or videotape a family member reciting the memory verse while others make the sound effects in the background.

## Living It
Have you ever seen an illustration of Noah's ark that showed the wicked people who were not on the boat? It is sad that they disobeyed God and were washed away. If we don't obey God, sometimes we can suffer great consequences. When Jesus told the parable of the houses built on rock and sand, he said, "Therefore everyone who hears these words of mine and puts them into practice is like a wise man who built his house on the rock" (Matthew 7:24). When a storm came, the house on the rock stood firm, but the house on the sand fell. Those who stand firm by hearing God's Word and putting it into practice will make it through any storm, or trouble, that life brings.

## Discussion Questions
◎ How are problems like storms?
◎ When you have gone through a hard time, how has obeying God kept you from getting into worse trouble?

## Prayer Prompter
Help us to listen to you and do what you say so that we will stand firm when storms arise.

# Don't Get Trapped
**Proverbs 11:1-6**

## Memory Verse
*The righteousness of the upright delivers them, but the unfaithful are trapped by evil desires (Proverbs 11:6).*

## Attention Grabber
Place a small toy figure or coin on top of a partially filled cup of sand, cornmeal, or sugar. Ask the kids what they know about quicksand. Shake the cup until the figure or coin disappears.

## Living It
Sin can be like quicksand: once we fall into it, it's hard to pull out of it. But believers can be made righteous (right with God) through Jesus. They can rely on him to help them have the strength to resist sin. Jesus says that "everyone who sins is a slave to sin" but he can set us free (John 8:34-36). First Corinthians 10:13 says, "God is faithful; he will not let you be tempted beyond what you can bear. But when you are tempted, he will also provide a way out so that you can stand up under it." When you're tempted, look for the way out that God has provided.

## Discussion Questions
◉ Why is it harder to resist a sin that you have committed repeatedly?
◉ How are evil desires like a trap?

## Prayer Prompter
Please show us how to break free from the sins we continue to repeat. When we're tempted, help us to see the way out that you have given us.

# Don't Laugh at Others
**Proverbs 11:7-12**

### Memory Verse

*A man who lacks judgment derides his neighbor, but a man of understanding holds his tongue (Proverbs 11:12).*

### Attention Grabber

Have the kids draw pictures of clowns. Or have each make a clown cone by putting a scoop of frozen yogurt or ice cream in a dish, placing a pointed ice cream cone on the scoop as a hat, and topping the point of the cone with a cherry. Then let each child make a clown face with candies and a tube of cake decorating icing. Emphasize that clowns like to be laughed at, but no one else does.

### Living It

To deride means to laugh at with hatred or disrespect. No one wants to be laughed at—except maybe clowns. Being laughed at is painful. Jesus talked about a person with a plank in his eye pointing out the sawdust in someone else's eye (Matthew 7:3) to remind us that sometimes when we're tempted to look down on others' flaws, we should look at our own flaws. We may have the same fault, only bigger!

### Discussion Questions

◉ How have you felt when people have laughed at you?
◉ When everyone teases one person in your class, what should you do?

### Prayer Prompter

Please help us to treat others with respect and resist when we're tempted to laugh at them.

# Secrets

## Proverbs 11:13-15

### Memory Verse
*A gossip betrays a confidence, but a trustworthy man keeps a secret (Proverbs 11:13).*

### Attention Grabber
Have everyone sit in a circle. Whisper the memory verse in the ear of the person sitting to your left and say, "Pass it on." See if the verse can make it all the way around the circle without the words getting jumbled.

### Living It
When a friend confides in you, she is trusting you. If you break that trust and gossip about your friend, she will be hurt and your relationship will be damaged. It's dishonest and disloyal to act like a friend and then gossip. But telling your parents about problems is not gossip. You should never keep secrets from your parents. They are there to help you. If you have a friend who is in trouble, tell your parents so they can help you decide what to do.

### Discussion Questions
- Who is a friend you can trust? Can your friends trust you? Why or why not?
- What are secrets kids might be tempted to keep from their parents? Why? What are the reasons it's important to tell parents anyway?
- What kinds of secrets would God want you to keep?

### Prayer Prompter
Please help us to be trustworthy and sensitive to others. Help us be open with our parents and trust them, too.

**Secrets**

# Be Kindhearted

## Memory Verse

*A kindhearted woman gains respect, but ruthless men gain only wealth (Proverbs 11:16).*

## Attention Grabber

Place a dollar bill in a chair. If you have two chenille stems, twist one near the top of the bill to form arms and another near the bottom of the bill to form legs. Explain that money does not make a good friend. It doesn't keep you company. It doesn't love you. It can't even talk. Emphasize that people matter much more than money.

## Living It

Some people will do anything to get rich, even if others get hurt in the process. They excuse the cruel way they treat others by saying, "That's business." A person who cares about others is more worthy of respect than a wealthy person who doesn't care about people.

## Discussion Questions

◉ What are ways some people take advantage of others to get rich or to win?

◉ Who are kindhearted people you know? How do they show that they have kind hearts?

## Prayer Prompter

Help us to remember that people matter much more than money.

# Kindness Has Benefits
**Proverbs 11:17-21**

## Memory Verse
*A kind man benefits himself, but a cruel man brings trouble on himself (Proverbs 11:17).*

## Attention Grabber
With your family's help, make a treat (such as Cake Mix Cookies on page 269) for a friend or neighbor. Double the recipe so you have enough for your family, too. Emphasize that this time you get to benefit right away from being kind to someone. Ask what the long-term blessings are.

## Living It
It must be hard for a cruel person to live with himself. It is unpleasant to think negative and mean thoughts. Kind people can enjoy their own company, and they are treated better by others. Sometimes kindness enriches friendships that bless the giver in the long run. Even if we don't receive anything in this life for being kind, we can be happy just knowing we've shown love to people and they are happier because of that. Jesus said, "It is more blessed to give than to receive" (Acts 20:35).

## Discussion Questions
◎ How have you been blessed because you did something kind for others?
◎ When you have treated others poorly, what has happened?

## Prayer Prompter
Help us to notice ways that you show us to be kind to others. Help us always to treat others well. Thank you for blessing us when we are kind.

# Good Judgment
**Proverbs 11:22, 23**

## Memory Verse
*Like a gold ring in a pig's snout is a beautiful woman who shows no discretion (Proverbs 11:22).*

## Attention Grabber
Show the kids a pretty piece of jewelry, such as a gold hoop earring or a gold chain. Then put the jewelry on in a silly way, such as wearing an earring on your nose. Or wear the jewelry while making an ugly face. Ask the kids how you look.

## Living It
Even if a person is physically beautiful, she will not be attractive if she doesn't exercise good judgment. Just like it is a ridiculous waste to put a valuable piece of jewelry on a farm animal, it is a waste for a person to be good-looking if there is no substance behind that appearance. Having the character to make wise choices is more important than being pretty or handsome.

## Discussion Questions
- How much time each day do you spend on your appearance? Can you spare at least that much time for prayer and Bible study?
- What are some examples of good judgment that you have seen others show recently?

## Prayer Prompter
Please develop wisdom in us so that we will have good judgment.

# Give and Receive

**Proverbs 11:24-27**

## Memory Verse

*A generous man will prosper; he who refreshes others will himself be refreshed (Proverbs 11:25).*

## Attention Grabber

Put a bag of flour and a bottle of oil on the table and then read 1 Kings 17:7-16 about the widow who shared her last meal of cake made from flour and oil with Elijah.

## Living It

When we give to others, we receive, too. Sometimes teachers say, "I learn even more than my students." As they study to help someone else learn, they learn themselves. If we try to cheer someone, we will usually feel better, too. The good we do for others comes back to us—sometimes immediately, sometimes later in life, and sometimes in heaven. God rewards us for whatever we do to help others (Ephesians 6:8).

## Discussion Questions

- What keeps you from being generous sometimes?
- In what ways have you helped others? How did you feel when you helped? What did you gain?

## Prayer Prompter

Please help us to be generous with our time, love, money, belongings, and everything else you give us.

# Thrive Like a Green Leaf
## Proverbs 11:28-31

## Memory Verse
*Whoever trusts in his riches will fall, but the righteous will thrive like a green leaf (Proverbs 11:28).*

## Attention Grabber
Show the kids a plant with both healthy and shriveled leaves. Emphasize that people who trust God are like the healthy leaves and those who trust their money are like the shriveled leaves. If you have time, let the kids write the memory verse on paper and make a border by arranging leaves under the edges of the paper and rubbing the paper with crayons.

## Living It
When we are right with God and trust him, he strengthens us. Those who trust their money and belongings instead of God will eventually find that their lives are empty, and they will fall like shriveled leaves. First Timothy 6:9, 10 says, "People who want to get rich fall into temptation and a trap and into many foolish and harmful desires that plunge men into ruin and destruction. For the love of money is a root of all kinds of evil. Some people, eager for money, have wandered from the faith and pierced themselves with many griefs." We need to fill our lives up with God, not with money or other things.

## Discussion Questions
- What can God do for you that riches can't?
- Are you content with what you have? Why or why not?

## Prayer Prompter
Thank you for Jesus, who makes us right with you. Help us to trust you and not our riches.

# Love Discipline
**Proverbs 12:1-3**

## Memory Verse
*Whoever loves discipline loves knowledge, but he who hates correction is stupid (Proverbs 12:1).*

## Attention Grabber
Use a red pen to make a list of corrections the kids tell you that teachers have written on their schoolwork. Discuss how the comments have helped them to learn.

## Living It
Just as you learn from the corrections teachers write on your papers, you need to learn from what God and your parents do to correct you. When you feel like God is trying to tell you to overcome a fault, yield to him. Let him change you. When your parents ask you to stop a behavior or start another one, obey. Try not to be angry when you have to be disciplined, because discipline can help you gain wisdom. No one wants to be stupid!

## Discussion Questions
◉ What is something you learned while being disciplined?
◉ Why do you have to be humble instead of proud to learn from correction?

## Prayer Prompter
Lord, please help us to be humble enough to learn when you and others correct and discipline us.

# Be a Crown
## Proverbs 12:4, 5

### Memory Verse

*A wife of noble character is her husband's crown, but a disgraceful wife is like decay in his bones (Proverbs 12:4).*

### Attention Grabber

Let the kids make pretend finger casts. Add drops of water to flour and mix until a paste forms. Dip gauze in the paste and then squeeze off as much paste as possible. Loosely wrap gauze around each child's index finger. Use a blow dryer to dry the "casts." If anyone has had a broken bone, have him tell what it feels like. Have the kids imagine what it would feel like to have decay in their bones.

### Living It

It would be very painful to have your bones rot, wouldn't it? It would feel like that to be married to someone who acts disgracefully. We wouldn't want to be a disgrace and make people miserable to be with us, either. It's important to be very careful and prayerful when entering into serious relationships with people, whether those relationships are friendships, business partnerships, or marriages. It's equally important for us to develop godly character so we can be prepared to be good friends, coworkers, or spouses. Second Peter 1:5-7 says to add the qualities of goodness, knowledge, self-control, perseverance, godliness, brotherly kindness, and love to our faith.

### Discussion Question

◉ What are examples for each of the character traits mentioned in 2 Peter 1:5-7? (For example, a person with faith trusts God, a person with goodness avoids what is evil, etc.)

### Prayer Prompter

Please develop noble character in us and help us to make good choices about our relationships with others.

# Pricey Popularity
**Proverbs 12:6-9**

## Memory Verse
*Better to be a nobody and yet have a servant than pretend to be somebody and have no food (Proverbs 12:9).*

## Attention Grabber
Ask the kids what it means to try to "keep up with the Joneses" (appear as wealthy as or wealthier than others). Pull cash and credit cards out of your wallet until it's empty and say, "If we spend all of our money on expensive belongings to impress people, we might not have enough for things that are more useful." Emphasize that someone who has spent all her money to look rich is actually not as rich as someone who has saved her money for what's more important.

## Living It
Sometimes people call getting rich "making something of your-self" or trying to "be somebody." You don't have to get rich to be somebody important to God. Get your confidence from the fact that God loves you rather than from your possessions. You should want people to like you for who you are, not for what you have. Spending a lot of money on things to try to impress others is a waste.

## Discussion Questions
- Do other people think you are rich? Why or why not?
- Have you ever bought an item to impress others (for example, a shirt with a special logo)? Why or why not?

## Prayer Prompter
Thank you for all that you give us, Lord. Please help us to be confident because of your love and not our belongings. Help us to use your resources wisely.

# Care for Animals

**Proverbs 12:10-12**

## Memory Verse

*A righteous man cares for the needs of his animal (Proverbs 12:10).*

## Attention Grabber

If you have a pet, make a pet care chart (grooming, feeding, watering, and walking) together with your family. Have the kids write the memory verse on paper and make a border of paw prints by pressing their fingers on an ink pad and putting three fingerprints above each thumbprint on the paper for each "paw."

## Living It

Animals belong to God (Psalm 50:10). We should treat them with kindness. Pets can't open the refrigerator or cabinets. They are totally dependent on their caregivers to make sure they don't miss a meal or run out of water.

## Discussion Questions

◉ What can you do to take care of animals?
◉ Why are some animals endangered and extinct?

## Prayer Prompter

Thank you for animals. Please help us to treat them with kindness.

# Fruit of Lips
**Proverbs 12:13, 14**

## Memory Verse

*From the fruit of his lips a man is filled with good things as surely as the work of his hands rewards him (Proverbs 12:14).*

## Attention Grabber

Cut unpeeled red apple slices or red Fruit Roll-Ups™ fruit rolls into lip shapes. Give them to the kids for a snack.

## Living It

The same way that working brings money to you, speaking kind words brings good things back to you. In general, if you are nice to people, they will like you. If you compliment them, they will probably smile and thank you. If you encourage them, it's likely they will want to be around you. If you write kind words in a letter or an e-mail, they will probably write you back. Speaking kindly to others also pleases God.

## Discussion Questions

- What are some compliments people have given to you? How did you respond?
- What are ways your words could express each of the fruit of the Spirit listed in Galatians 5:22, 23?

## Prayer Prompter

Please guide our words so that they will express the fruit of the Spirit.

# Listen to Advice

**Proverbs 12:15**

## Memory Verse

*The way of a fool seems right to him, but a wise man listens to advice (Proverbs 12:15).*

## Attention Grabber

Have everyone write short letters asking advice for problems and sign the letters with anonymous names like Confused in California or Troubled in Toronto. Read the letters aloud and have everyone give advice.

## Living It

It isn't wise to make up your mind before listening to what other people think. Sometimes others may mention points you haven't considered. It's important to get your advice from people who follow God. And it's very important to check any advice against God's Word to make sure the advice is good.

## Discussion Questions

- When have you thought you were right about something and then were surprised to find out you were wrong?
- Who could you ask for good advice? Why would you choose that person?

## Prayer Prompter

Help us to ask people we respect for advice and to consider their opinions before making our decisions.

# Overlook Insults
**Proverbs 12:16, 17**

## Memory Verse
*A fool shows his annoyance at once, but a prudent man overlooks an insult (Proverbs 12:16).*

## Attention Grabber
If you have time, let the kids make duck-shaped soaps by mixing three drops of yellow food coloring, two tablespoons of warm water, and one and a half cups of Ivory Snow™ laundry detergent flakes together and shaping the mixture into duck shapes. Or have the kids imitate ducks. Emphasize that we should let insults slide off our backs as easily as water runs off of a duck's back.

## Living It
When someone insults or annoys you, it's wise to stay calm and try not to be offended. Sometimes people aren't even trying to bother you; they may have just chosen their words poorly. Other people may be trying to upset you; if you ignore their insults, they may quit. First Peter 3:9 says, "Do not repay evil with evil or insult with insult, but with blessing, because to this you were called so that you may inherit a blessing." Paul said, "When we are cursed, we bless; when we are persecuted, we endure it; when we are slandered, we answer kindly" (1 Corinthians 4:12, 13).

## Discussion Questions
- Have you ever hurt someone's feelings unintentionally? What happened?
- Everyone gets teased sometimes. How do you keep it from bothering you?

## Prayer Prompter
Please help us respond to people with love even when they haven't treated us that way.

# Words Hurt or Heal
**Proverbs 12:18-24**

## Memory Verse

*Reckless words pierce like a sword, but the tongue of the wise brings healing (Proverbs 12:18).*

## Attention Grabber

Cut the shape of a person out of poster board or stiff cardboard. As you poke holes in the cutout with a pushpin, explain that what we say to people can be very painful to them. Rub the holes closed or put adhesive bandage strips over them, and explain that our words can also heal people's pain.

## Living It

When we talk to people, it's important to remember that our words affect them. Just as people have physical feelings, they have emotional feelings. Just as stabbing someone causes tremendous pain, words can cause tremendous pain, too. It's important to think carefully before we speak so that our words heal instead of hurt.

## Discussion Questions

- What does a reckless driver do? How is a reckless talker like that?
- When your feelings have been hurt, what are some things people have said that made you feel better?

## Prayer Prompter

Help us to think before we speak so that our words heal instead of hurt.

# Kind Words Cheer

**Proverbs 12:25-28**

## Memory Verse

*An anxious heart weighs a man down, but a kind word cheers him up (Proverbs 12:25).*

## Attention Grabber

Show the kids uninflated balloons that represent discouraged friends. Let them blow up the balloons and draw smiling faces on them.

## Living It

When people are discouraged, sometimes they say, "She took the wind out of my sails" or "He burst my bubble" or "What he said let the air out of my tires." Our words can either deflate people or fill them up. God wants us to use our words to encourage others.

## Discussion Questions

- ◎ Who do you expect to see today or tomorrow? What can you say that will cheer them?
- ◎ What prevents you from telling others how much you like them, care about them, and admire them?

## Prayer Prompter

Please use us to cheer others.

# Walk With the Wise
**Proverbs 13:1-20**

## Memory Verse

*He who walks with the wise grows wise, but a companion of fools suffers harm (Proverbs 13:20).*

## Attention Grabber

Have the kids wash their hands, but make sure they don't dry them thoroughly. Put some colored candies in their hands and have them close their hands for a minute or so. Emphasize that just as the colors of the candies rub off onto their hands, their friends will "rub off" on them. If you don't have candies, use paper towels cut into people shapes. Put a drop of food coloring on one shape, and then touch it with another to show how the color spreads.

## Living It

Even though we are supposed to love everyone, we must be careful about who we spend a great deal of time with because they will influence us. Proverbs 12:26 says, "A righteous man is cautious in friendship." Proverbs 22:24, 25 says, "Do not make friends with a hot-tempered man, do not associate with one easily angered, or you may learn his ways and get yourself ensnared." Be sure to choose friends that you want to be like, because they will rub off on you.

## Discussion Questions

◎ Of the people you know who are your age, who do you admire the most? Are they your friends? Why or why not?
◎ What good and bad traits have you already picked up from your friends?

## Prayer Prompter

Please show us the people you want us to have as friends, and help us to obey when you want us to avoid friendships that have a bad influence on us.

# Don't Spare the Rod
## Proverbs 13:21-25

### Memory Verse
*He who spares the rod hates his son, but he who loves him is careful to discipline him (Proverbs 13:24).*

### Attention Grabber
Tell the kids a misbehavior for which your parents punished you. Explain how the discipline helped you, and explain that if your parents hadn't loved you, they would have just ignored you and let you grow up to be a person who still misbehaved that way.

### Living It
It can be easier in some ways for parents to ignore their kids' misbehavior than to correct it. It's unpleasant to correct children and punish them. But parents show love when they take the time and energy to discipline so that their children can learn right from wrong and avoid the consequences of bad character.

### Discussion Questions
◉ What kind of discipline do you learn from the best?
◉ Do the rules in your house seem too strict, too relaxed, or just right? Why?

### Prayer Prompter
Please help us make good decisions about discipline. Help us to learn from the times when we are punished. Help us to know that we are always loved.

# Build Your House
## Proverbs 14:1-8

### Memory Verse

*The wise woman builds her house, but with her own hands the foolish one tears hers down (Proverbs 14:1).*

### Attention Grabber

Beforehand, obtain a large cardboard box. When it's your devotion time, work together with the kids to transform the box into a playhouse. Cut out windows and doors. Let the kids tape fabric scraps to it for curtains, and draw flowers, bricks, and pictures for the walls. Write the memory verse on the house.

### Living It

This memory verse isn't talking about building a house with a hammer; it's about building up your family with kind words and taking care of your household. A foolish person tears down her family members with criticism and insults. A wise person builds up her family members with encouragement and praise. If your family feels good, it's easier for you to feel good, too. A positive atmosphere also makes it easier for everyone to do what needs to be done. God wants us to be wise and to love one another.

### Discussion Questions

- Why would it be unwise to tear down your house? Why would it be unwise to tear down your family?
- What is the most encouraging thing a family member has said to you recently?

### Prayer Prompter

Help us to build up all of the members of our family.

# Make Amends
## Proverbs 14:9-11

### Memory Verse
*Fools mock at making amends for sin, but goodwill is found among the upright (Proverbs 14:9).*

### Attention Grabber
Put a small candy bar on the table. Ask, "If you had this candy bar and someone stole it, how would you feel?" Put a large candy bar on the table. Ask, "If that person apologized and replaced it with this candy bar, how would you feel?" Explain that a wise person would forgive, but a foolish person might tease the person for apologizing and trying to repair the damaged friendship.

### Living It
When you have done something wrong, it is good to try to fix whatever you can about the situation. Sometimes people will praise you for this, and sometimes foolish people may tease you for it. Either way, it is important to apologize. It is right and good to say you are sorry. It is also good to be quick to forgive those who apologize to you and to remember that apologizing isn't easy for anyone.

### Discussion Questions
- Have you ever felt guilty about something and then tried to correct what you had done wrong? What happened?
- When a person apologizes, is it tempting to "rub it in" before forgiving? Why or why not?

### Prayer Prompter
Please forgive our sins and show us how to do whatever we can to repair the damage we have caused. Also, help us to be quick to forgive those who have wronged us.

# What's Right?
## Proverbs 14:12-14

## Memory Verse

*There is a way that seems right to a man, but in the end it leads to death (Proverbs 14:12).*

## Attention Grabber

Cut three pieces of string or yarn. Tie knots in two of the pieces and show the pieces to the kids. Mix up the pieces and hide the knots in your fist or under a piece of paper. Can the kids guess which is the unknotted string? Explain that even when people feel sure about something, they might be wrong.

## Living It

It can be easy for people to believe things that aren't true. It is important to read the Bible so we know what's right. Otherwise, we might believe something that isn't true. Some people judge what's right by what laws say or by what most people do. But the way to know what is truly right is by reading what God says and talking to him.

## Discussion Questions

- What are beliefs some people have that are not in the Bible?
- In addition to family devotions, are you doing personal Bible study daily? Why or why not? What would help you make daily Bible reading a habit?

## Prayer Prompter

Help us to know your Word, so that we know the truth.

# Plan Your Steps
Proverbs 14:15-19

### Memory Verse
*A simple man believes anything, but a prudent man gives thought to his steps (Proverbs 14:15).*

### Attention Grabber
On an uncooked lasagna noodle, write "Use your noodle!" Ask the kids what that means. Explain that this saying means to use your brain—to think carefully about your actions. Or show the kids chess pieces and emphasize that to win a chess game, you must plan several moves in advance before you make each move.

### Living It
God gave you a big brain and he wants you to use it! Don't just do what other people are doing or believe what others say. Carefully think about things before you say, do, or believe in anything. Consider what the results of your actions will be. Remember to check with God to see what he has to say about what you should do.

### Discussion Questions
- Do you believe everything you hear on TV? Why or why not?
- What are examples of things others have told you to do that were not the best choice?

### Prayer Prompter
Thank you for our brains and the ability to think. Please guide us and help us to think carefully so that we will take the right steps.

# Kind to the Needy
**Proverbs 14:20, 21**

## Memory Verse

*He who despises his neighbor sins, but blessed is he who is kind to the needy (Proverbs 14:21).*

## Attention Grabber

On a blanket (preferably blue or green), draw a circle with chalk to represent the earth. Wrap the blanket around yourself and say, "Sometimes we get wrapped up in our own little world."

## Living It

God wants us to look beyond ourselves and our small circle of family and friends. He wants us to love other people, too. He wants us to care about the needs of the people who live down the street from us, the people who are across the country from us, and even the people who are across the world from us.

## Discussion Questions

◉ Some people hate others who are different from them. How can they overcome this hatred?

◉ What can you and your family do to help the needy? (You might want to write these ideas on the calendar.)

## Prayer Prompter

Thank you for blessing us so generously. Help us to reach out and show love beyond our small circle of family and friends.

# Work Brings Profit
**Proverbs 14:22-29**

## Memory Verse
*All hard work brings a profit, but mere talk leads only to poverty (Proverbs 14:23).*

## Attention Grabber
Give the children simple, quick jobs (dusting shelves, putting away dishes, etc.) they can do to earn money and then encourage them to get to work. Explain that just talking about the work doesn't put the money in their hands. After they are finished, give them their payment and continue with the devotion.

## Living It
Planning and preparation are good, but it's important to get down to work. God doesn't want us to sit around and be idle. First Thessalonians 4:11, 12 says, "Make it your ambition to lead a quiet life, to mind your own business and to work with your hands, just as we told you, so that your daily life may win the respect of outsiders and so that you will not be dependent on anybody." Working hard can bring us money, but it also shows others that we, as Christians, are responsible and that we can be trusted to do a good job.

## Discussion Questions
- Are you a hard worker? What shows this?
- In addition to money, what are the benefits of hard work?
- Think of a time when you enjoyed working hard. What made it fun?

## Prayer Prompter
Please help us to be hard workers and to do what we say we will do.

# A Heart at Peace
### Proverbs 14:30-35

## Memory Verse

*A heart at peace gives life to the body, but envy rots the bones (Proverbs 14:30).*

## Attention Grabber

Beforehand, cut four large hearts out of paper for each family member. Tell your family to use crayons to illustrate each of these four emotions, using one heart for each emotion: anger, jealousy, love, and peace. (For example, someone might draw an angry face or black lightning bolts on a heart for anger, and a dove or calm blue sea on a heart for peace.)

## Living It

When you have a negative feeling, such as envy, that feeling can create harmful chemicals in your body. Sometimes stress (feeling pressured) can even make you sick. It is important to give our negative feelings to God. Instead of being jealous, we can pray for others and be glad when good things happen to them. Instead of being angry, we can ask God to help us forgive. Not only will doing this help the other person feel better, it will help us feel better, too!

## Discussion Questions

- Have you ever felt hot when you were angry or had a stomachache when you were scared? What are other responses your body has had to emotions?
- How does going to God give you peace?

## Prayer Prompter

God, take our negative feelings from us. Help us to forgive others. Help us learn to be at peace with you, with others, and with ourselves.

# A Gentle Answer
**Proverbs 15:1-7**

## Memory Verse

*A gentle answer turns away wrath, but a harsh word stirs up anger (Proverbs 15:1).*

## Attention Grabber

Beforehand, heat some water in a pot until it begins to boil. Explain that when someone is "boiling mad" at you, you can make the situation worse by saying harsh things (turn up the heat so the boiling is more intense) or you can give a gentle answer that calms the person (turn off the heat so the boiling ceases).

## Living It

Romans 12:18 says, "If it is possible, as far as it depends on you, live at peace with everyone." There is a lot we can do to settle disagreements quickly. When someone is angry with you, try to stay calm. Instead of getting angry yourself and saying something that will only make the person feel more angry, apologize or say something kind that will help calm the person.

## Discussion Questions

- What are examples of harsh and gentle ways to answer an accusation?
- What does it mean to "get defensive"? Is it good to do that? Why or why not?

## Prayer Prompter

Help us to be humble enough to settle arguments quickly. Give us wisdom about what to say that will calm others.

**A Gentle Answer**

# What's Better
## Proverbs 15:8-16

## Memory Verse
*Better a little with the fear of the Lord than great wealth with turmoil (Proverbs 15:16).*

## Attention Grabber
Stick pieces of masking tape on fourteen coins (the coins can be all different sizes). Write one word from the memory verse on the tape on each of the coins, using all the words. Mix up the coins and put them in a pile on the table or floor. Have the kids work together to put the words of the verse in the correct order.

## Living It
Fearing the Lord means having reverence for him, having great respect and awe for his power and majesty. If you know God, you don't need a lot of money, because God can give you whatever you need. There are many wealthy people who don't know God and are very worried people. It's better to have a good relationship with God than to have great wealth.

## Discussion Questions
◉ Why might you feel worried if you didn't know God?
◉ Why is it sometimes more difficult for wealthy people to follow God?

## Prayer Prompter
We worship you, Lord. You are mighty and powerful. Help us to trust you rather than money.

# A Meal With Love
**Proverb 15:17**

## Memory Verse
*Better a meal of vegetables where there is love than a fattened calf with hatred (Proverbs 15:17).*

## Attention Grabber
Let the kids arrange vegetables on a platter and make a simple vegetable dip (or pour salad dressing into a bowl for a dip).

## Living It
In Bible times, a fattened calf would have been considered quite a feast for a family. It is better to have a simple lifestyle and a loving attitude than to have great riches and terrible relationships. Our relationships with our family and other people matter much more than how much money we have.

## Discussion Questions
◉ When you're older, do you plan on making lots of money? Why or why not? How might working long hours hurt your family relationships?
◉ What kinds of arguments do families have about money? How can these be avoided?

## Prayer Prompter
Thank you for the love that is in our family. Please unite us even more, and help us to be satisfied with all you have provided for us.

**A Meal With Love**

# Calm a Quarrel
## Proverbs 15:18-21

### Memory Verse

*A hot-tempered man stirs up dissension, but a patient man calms a quarrel (Proverbs 15:18).*

### Attention Grabber

Prick holes in a potato and microwave it for about eight minutes. (You only need one for the devotion, but you might want to cook more potatoes to serve with assorted toppings for dinner.) Wrap a dish towel around the potato and pass the wrapped spud from person to person when it is not too hot. Point out that the heat of the potato radiates through the towel and warms our hands. Emphasize that our emotions radiate to other people, too.

### Living It

You affect the people around you. If you have a hot temper, you may cause others to feel like arguing. If you are calm, you may help others to settle down. A patient person is not annoyed easily by other people. When someone is angry with you, that doesn't mean you have to get angry. Stay calm and don't argue or yell. You increase the chances of coming to an agreement if you show that you are listening and trying to understand the other viewpoint. If you listen, the other person may listen, too. If either of you are too upset for that, it might be best to suggest that you talk after you are both calm. God wants us to treat people with love. First Corinthians 13:4, 5 says that love is patient and is not easily angered.

### Discussion Questions

◎ Who do you know who is patient? How does that person react when others are upset?
◎ In what situations do you need to be more patient?

### Prayer Prompter

Please help us to be patient and to have a calming effect on others.

# Successful Plans
**Proverbs 15:22**

---

### Memory Verse
*Plans fail for lack of counsel, but with many advisers they succeed (Proverbs 15:22).*

### Attention Grabber
Before the devotion, clip out the activities calendar from the newspaper. Plan a simple family outing together. Ask everyone's opinions about when you should leave, what you should bring, what activities you should include, etc. Ask why it was helpful to have everyone's input.

### Living It
When you have plans to make, it's helpful to have others' input for many reasons. They might have good ideas that hadn't occurred to you. They might be able to warn you about problems that are preventable. Getting others' input helps them feel more involved, which makes them enjoy the experience more, too. Asking for their advice also shows that you respect them.

### Discussion Questions
◉ How could pride keep you from asking for others' opinions?
◉ What good advice have you received from family and friends?

### Prayer Prompter
Help us to be humble enough to ask for advice.

# A Timely Word
## Proverbs 15:23-33

## Memory Verse
*A man finds joy in giving an apt reply—and how good is a timely word! (Proverbs 15:23).*

## Attention Grabber
Role-play some serious situations about which your children may have to counsel their friends (for example, a friend saying she feels sick, her parents are divorcing, her grandmother died, she's moving, etc.).

## Living It
An "apt" reply is the right thing to say at the right time. Sometimes hard situations take us by surprise and it's hard to know what to say. But we can prepare for those times by trying to understand God's Word more now and by examining our hearts daily, because "out of the overflow of the heart the mouth speaks" (Matthew 12:34). It's also important to listen for the Holy Spirit's guidance about what to say.

## Discussion Questions
◎ What is an example of an apt reply that you have given to someone? What was that person's response?
◎ If friends need to talk, why should we try to find time for them right then if we can?

## Prayer Prompter
Help us to give the right responses at the right time. Help us to be available to our friends when they need us.

# God Weighs Motives

**Proverbs 16:1, 2**

 ## Memory Verse

*All a man's ways seem innocent to him, but motives are weighed by the Lord (Proverbs 16:2).*

 ## Attention Grabber

Hold a magnifying glass, microscope, or eyeglasses over your daily planner or calendar. Pretend to examine it and say, "Everything I'm doing looks good." Look at your arms and legs through the glass and say, "Yes, everything about me seems just right." Explain that people often think that whatever they're thinking, doing, and saying is right.

 ## Living It

Even when criminals are interviewed in jail, they will often defend their actions as right. Sometimes people are not able to see themselves very accurately. It's important to ask God to examine our hearts and show us what we need to change. Our motives are our reasons for our actions. Jesus wants us to do good out of love for him and other people, not because we want others to admire us or for other selfish reasons. You can trust that if you ask God to cleanse your heart, he will do it with gentleness and love.

 ## Discussion Question

⊚ What would be a good motive for giving an apple or a flower to your teacher? What would be a bad motive? (Expand on this with other examples of good deeds.)

 ## Prayer Prompter

Please show us our hearts as they truly are. Cleanse our hearts, and help us to do good for others purely out of love for them and you.

# Commit to God

## Memory Verse

*Commit to the Lord whatever you do, and your plans will succeed (Proverbs 16:3).*

## Attention Grabber

Use an ottoman or small table to represent an altar. Put objects representing different parts of your life (for example, a wedding ring for marriage, a house key for care of your home, an agenda or other work-related object for your career) on the altar. Tell the kids that you have committed these things to God or that you want to do that.

## Living It

To commit what you do to the Lord means several things. First, you need to make sure it's what he wants you to do. Trust that he will help you, and tell him you will do the best you can. Then do it for him, giving him control over your actions. We need to look at our lives closely to see if there is anything we are trying to control without God's help. We need to commit to the Lord everything we do, no matter how big or small.

## Discussion Questions

⊙ What do you need to commit to the Lord? How can you commit your schoolwork to the Lord?

⊙ When you are deciding what to be when you grow up, how can you commit that decision to the Lord?

## Prayer Prompter

We want you to be Lord over everything we do. Please help us to commit our whole lives to you.

# Pride Before a Fall
**Proverbs 16:18-22**

## Memory Verse
*Pride goes before destruction, a haughty spirit before a fall (Proverbs 16:18).*

## Attention Grabber
Have the kids stack checkers or coins in a tower until the tower falls. Compare building this tower to someone who praises himself for every good thing he does but looks down on others.

## Living It
If we are prideful and think that we are better than others or that we don't need God's help or forgiveness, God will let something humble us. In Luke 18:14, Jesus said that "everyone who exalts himself will be humbled, and he who humbles himself will be exalted." First Corinthians 10:12 warns, "So, if you think you are standing firm, be careful that you don't fall!"

## Discussion Questions
◉ How can you feel good about yourself without being prideful? (recognize that you are righteous through Jesus rather than because of your own good works, acknowledge that your gifts and talents come from him, etc.)
◉ What is the difference between being confident and being prideful?

## Prayer Prompter
Help us to be humble and recognize how much we need you.

# Pleasant Words
## Proverbs 16:23-33

### Memory Verse
*Pleasant words are a honeycomb, sweet to the soul and healing to the bones (Proverbs 16:24).*

### Attention Grabber
Let each child make a candle by rolling a small square sheet of beehive candle wax (from a craft store) around a wick. Or serve crackers with honey from a jar of honey that contains a piece of honeycomb.

### Living It
Many people have hard lives and do not get a lot of praise and encouragement from the people around them. Pleasant words can add sweetness to their lives and may even help them feel better about themselves and show them God's love.

### Discussion Questions
◉ What are some sweet things you have heard family members and friends say recently?
◉ Do you want to be a sweet person? Why or why not?

### Prayer Prompter
Please help us to keep our words sweet.

# God Tests the Heart
**Proverbs 17:1-21**

## Memory Verse

*The crucible for silver and the furnace for gold, but the Lord tests the heart (Proverbs 17:3).*

## Attention Grabber

Have the kids see how many jumping jacks they can do. Emphasize that if they exercised this way often, their hearts would grow stronger and they could do more jumping jacks. Ask them if a physical education teacher has ever tested their level of physical fitness by having them do jumping jacks and other exercises.

## Living It

Exercise strengthens our hearts physically. Trials strengthen our hearts spiritually. First Peter 1:6 says we "suffer grief in all kinds of trials" so that our faith, which is of greater worth than gold "may be proved genuine and may result in praise, glory and honor when Jesus Christ is revealed." When we are having troubles, if we turn to Jesus for help, we see how faithful he is to answer our prayers. That helps our faith to become stronger and more pure. After we exercise our bodies for a while, a physical education instructor can test us to see if our hearts are physically stronger. As we go through trials, God can test us to see if our hearts are growing spiritually stronger.

## Discussion Questions

◉ What are some trials you have faced? How did God help you through them?
◉ What have you learned from your trials?

## Prayer Prompter

Help us to trust you to keep us strong in our trials and to use them to help us grow.

# A Cheerful Heart

### Memory Verse

*A cheerful heart is good medicine, but a crushed spirit dries up the bones (Proverbs 17:22).*

### Attention Grabber

Beforehand, for each family member write a pretend prescription that says "Rx: a cheerful heart." Fill a glass half full of whatever drink you have on hand. Ask the kids if the glass is half full or half empty. Emphasize that a situation may be good or bad depending on how you look at it. Give each family member a prescription for a cheerful heart.

### Living It

Having a cheerful attitude prevents stress and helps us to stay healthy. Whatever we consider bad news can almost always be considered good news if we look at it another way. We need to trust that God has a good purpose for everything that happens to us, even if we can't see the benefit right away. When Joseph's brothers tried to harm him by selling him as a slave, it seemed that Joseph would have a terrible life. But eventually God used Joseph to save many people from starving to death (Genesis 50:20).

### Discussion Questions

- What cheers you when you're in a bad mood?
- Can you remember the time you laughed the hardest? What were you laughing about? Did the laughter make you feel better?

### Prayer Prompter

Please help us to stay cheerful and see situations positively.

# The Quiet Seem Wise
## Proverbs 17:25-28

### Memory Verse
*Even a fool is thought wise if he keeps silent, and discerning if he holds his tongue (Proverbs 17:28).*

### Attention Grabber
Have the kids do a simple skit in which one person speaks rapidly about something ridiculously trivial while the other person eventually dozes and then falls off his seat. Point out that it is possible to talk too much.

### Living It
It is important to be a good listener so that we fully understand what other people are trying to tell us. We should think before we talk so that we don't say what is meaningless or wrong. People respect those who choose their words carefully.

### Discussion Questions
- How do you know when you should speak up and when you should remain quiet?
- Who do you know who is respected because he is quiet?

### Prayer Prompter
Help us to have the wisdom to wait to speak until we have something worthwhile to say.

# Gossip Morsels

**Proverbs 18:1-8**

## Memory Verse

*The words of a gossip are like choice morsels; they go down to a man's inmost parts (Proverbs 18:8).*

## Attention Grabber

Give each family member a semisweet chocolate chip. After all family members have eaten the chocolate, ask if you can have the chips back. When they say no, emphasize that of course you can't have the chips back because the chocolate has been swallowed and is now a part of their bodies.

## Living It

If we gossip, others may be as interested in hearing what we say as they would be if we were offering sweets. And they might crave more gossip. Gossip is often filled with bad or false messages. If we pass these messages along to other people, those people will have those bad and false thoughts in their heads. Also, by passing on these messages, we may damage someone's reputation. We can't take back our words. The damage is already done once the words leave our mouths. Even if what we are gossiping about is true, it is still wrong to talk about things that are not our business.

## Discussion Questions

- How have you felt when you found out someone gossiped about you? How did it harm you?
- When people start to gossip, how can you stop them without hurting their feelings?

## Prayer Prompter

Please help us not to gossip or listen to the gossip of others.

# A Strong Tower
**Proverbs 18:9-11**

### Memory Verse
*The name of the Lord is a strong tower; the righteous run to it and are safe (Proverbs 18:10).*

### Attention Grabber
Give everyone modeling clay to form into small "bricks." Let the kids arrange the bricks to form a tower. Emphasize that during battles, soldiers who were inside towers were safe from arrows, swords, and spears.

### Living It
We're in a battle against evil (Ephesians 6:12), but we are safe if we run to the Lord. We tend to rely on God more when we feel weak, so in that way, feeling weak is actually good. In 2 Corinthians 12:10, Paul says, "That is why, for Christ's sake, I delight in weaknesses, in insults, in hardships, in persecutions, in difficulties. For when I am weak, then I am strong." We are safe and strong, like soldiers in a tower, when we rely on Jesus.

### Discussion Questions
◉ How does knowing that Jesus is with you make you feel strong?
◉ When you're in trouble, do you run to God right away? Why or why not?

### Prayer Prompter
Thank you for being a safe place for us. Thank you for protecting us.

**A Strong Tower**

# A Wife Is Good
**Proverbs 18:12-22**

 ## Memory Verse
*He who finds a wife finds what is good and receives favor from the Lord (Proverbs 18:22).*

 ## Attention Grabber
Sing or play "The Farmer in the Dell." Stop right after "the farmer takes a wife," and say, "That was a good thing."

 ## Living It
God gave Adam a wife because it wasn't good for him to be alone (Genesis 2:18). Marriage is holy because God joins the husband and wife together (Matthew 19:5, 6). Husbands and wives should never take their spouses for granted. If you marry, your spouse will be one of your greatest blessings. But if you don't marry, that doesn't mean you don't have God's favor. God blesses everyone in different ways.

 ## Discussion Questions
◉ How is having a spouse a good thing?
◉ If you were married, what ways would you show your spouse how glad you were to be together?

 ## Prayer Prompter
Help us to treat others well and to appreciate the blessings you give us, Lord. And if we marry or if we are already married, help us to have good marriages.

# Close Friends
**Proverbs 18:23, 24**

 ## Memory Verse
*A man of many companions may come to ruin, but there is a friend who sticks closer than a brother (Proverbs 18:24).*

 ## Attention Grabber
Have each kid make a friendship pin by putting several beads on a safety pin or make a friendship bracelet by braiding together strands of embroidery floss. Or have the kids think of ways they can let their closest friends know how much they appreciate their friendship.

 ## Living It
True friendship rather than popularity should be our goal. A friend loves you for who you really are. A fan only likes you if you're wearing and doing what's "cool" at the moment. Fans are fickle; their loyalty can change quickly, but a true friend will be there for you during good times and bad. Jesus says he is our friend (John 15:15).

 ## Discussion Questions
- What are the qualities of a true friend? How does God show those qualities to you?
- Who are your closest friends? Why?

 ## Prayer Prompter
Thank you for being a true friend to us and for giving us good friends. Please help us to be a true friend to them and you.

# Not So Fast
## Proverbs 19:1, 2

## Memory Verse
*It is not good to have zeal without knowledge, nor to be hasty and miss the way (Proverbs 19:2).*

## Attention Grabber
Ask the kids if they've ever had dreams in which they went to school wearing their pajamas. Or ask if they've ever rushed home and forgotten to bring their homework with them. Ask what the saying "Haste makes waste" means.

## Living It
It's great to be excited about opportunities, but it's important to take time to look ahead and prepare for them rather than rushing into things too quickly. Study the Bible before rushing out to teach people what the Bible says. Know someone well and pray before you get married. Pray sincerely about how God wants you to serve him instead of rushing off to serve your own way. Remember what Psalm 127:1 says? "Unless the Lord builds the house, its builders labor in vain." We're wasting our time if we're not doing what God wants or if we try to do it without preparation.

## Discussion Questions
- When have you rushed into something without being prepared? What happened?
- Do you already have an idea of what God might have planned for your life and how he wants you to prepare? What do you think he wants you to do?

## Prayer Prompter
We are excited to serve you, Lord, but please help us to take time to listen for your direction and to prepare well.

# Not God's Fault
## Proverbs 19:3-8

### Memory Verse

*A man's own folly ruins his life, yet his heart rages against the Lord (Proverbs 19:3).*

### Attention Grabber

Beforehand, ask a family member to pretend to walk into a wall at the beginning of devotion time (by kicking the baseboard and then holding her head) and to say, "Dumb old wall!" After she does this, explain that it isn't the wall's fault if we walk into it.

### Living It

When we are hurt, it's common to want to blame something or someone. Unfortunately, some people blame God for things that are their own fault. Foolish actions have consequences. When we make poor choices, we need to accept responsibility for them. After all, God is perfect, so he can't be at fault.

### Discussion Questions

- ◉ What are some choices that have bad consequences?
- ◉ When you're hurting, why is it smarter to ask for God's help than to blame him?

### Prayer Prompter

When we hurt, help us remember to turn to you for help instead of blaming you.

# Lend to the Lord
## Proverbs 19:9-17

## Memory Verse

*He who is kind to the poor lends to the Lord, and he will reward him for what he has done (Proverbs 19:17).*

## Attention Grabber

Remind the kids of a time someone helped them. Emphasize that because you love your children, you appreciated that help as much as if someone had done that for you.

## Living It

God loves his children, so when we help them, it's as if we are helping God. Jesus told his disciples that one day he'll tell people who have helped others, "'I tell you the truth, whatever you did for one of the least of these brothers of mine, you did for me'" (Matthew 25:40).

## Discussion Questions

- In Matthew 25:34-40, what are some of the ways that the righteous helped people?
- How do you feel when you donate to charity? Why?

## Prayer Prompter

Help us to treat the poor as well as we want to treat you.

# Discipline and Hope
**Proverbs 19:18, 19**

## Memory Verse

*Discipline your son, for in that there is hope; do not be a willing party to his death (Proverbs 19:18).*

## Attention Grabber

Have the kids list forms of discipline and rank them in order of preference. Discuss why they feel the way they do.

## Living It

It's important for parents to discipline their children. Not only does discipline help children to grow up to be better people, it can even save their lives. For example, giving a child strict rules about not handling matches and punishing him when he disobeys those rules may help him avoid starting a fire that could harm people or even kill them.

## Discussion Questions

- How does disciplining you show that your parents have hope for you?
- If your parents discipline you well, what can they hope about you?

## Prayer Prompter

Help us to learn from discipline and to realize it helps us. If we have children ourselves, help us to discipline them well, with love.

# Listen and Be Wise
**Proverbs 19:20-29**

## Memory Verse

*Listen to advice and accept instruction, and in the end you will be wise (Proverbs 19:20).*

## Attention Grabber

Give the kids modeling clay and let them make ears that are oversized or look like Vulcan ears. Have them put the clay ears over their ears. Discuss what it means to say, "I'm all ears."

## Living It

Jesus often said "whoever has ears to hear, let him hear." Most people have ears, but we don't all listen with them. If we want to gain wisdom, we need to listen and accept advice and instruction. Life is too short for us to learn all of our own lessons the hard way—on our own.

## Discussion Questions

◉ Whose instruction and advice do you need to take?
◉ How has the instruction or advice of others helped you already?

## Prayer Prompter

Please help us learn to listen to the advice and instruction of those who are wiser than we are. Help us listen to you, especially.

# Dangers of Drinking

**Proverbs 20:1**

## Memory Verse

*Wine is a mocker and beer a brawler; whoever is led astray by them is not wise (Proverbs 20:1).*

## Attention Grabber

Stick a strip of masking tape on the floor. Have the kids walk along the line. Explain that police make drunk drivers try to walk in a straight line, and sometimes the drivers can't even do that.

## Living It

Mockers try to make people look foolish; wine can make a person act foolishly. It can also cause the drinker to make fun of others. Brawlers are fighters; beer can make people get in fights or look and feel like they have been in a fight. Ephesians 5:18 says, "Do not get drunk on wine, which leads to debauchery. Instead, be filled with the Spirit." It's important not to be out of control.

## Discussion Questions

- What are problems that are caused by people getting drunk?
- How is being filled with the Spirit better than being drunk?

## Prayer Prompter

Please help us to understand the harmful effects of drinking too much.

# Avoid Arguments
## Proverbs 20:2, 3

### Memory Verse
*It is to a man's honor to avoid strife, but every fool is quick to quarrel (Proverbs 20:3).*

### Attention Grabber
Mention one or two situations that cause frequent conflicts in your family, such as who gets the window seat in the car or the largest piece of dessert. Help the kids come up with ways to solve the problems without arguments.

### Living It
A fool tries to solve problems by arguing and fighting. God wants us to work things out in ways that show love to the people around us. Philippians 2:14 says, "Do everything without complaining or arguing."

### Discussion Questions
- How does quarreling with someone make you feel? How does it make the other person feel?
- How can you become easier to get along with?

### Prayer Prompter
Please help us learn to solve our disagreements without quarreling.

# Be Faithful
## Proverbs 20:4-10

### Memory Verse
*Many a man claims to have unfailing love, but a faithful man who can find? (Proverbs 20:6).*

### Attention Grabber
Cut out hearts and have everyone write on her heart, "I will show love to God this week by faithfully _____." (Let each person fill in the blank). Have each child tape the heart to a place where it can be a reminder.

### Living It
Jesus said, "If you love me, you will obey what I command" (John 14:15). We show our love by faithfully doing what God has said. First John 5:3 says, "This is love for God: to obey his commands. And his commands are not burdensome." It's not enough to say we love him; we need to show it. First John 4:20, 21 says, "If anyone says, 'I love God,' yet hates his brother, he is a liar. For anyone who does not love his brother, whom he has seen, cannot love God, whom he has not seen. And he has given us this command: Whoever loves God must also love his brother."

### Discussion Questions
◉ What are some ways you show your love to God?
◉ In what ways do you feel God would like you to show your love for him more?

### Prayer Prompter
Thank you for giving us commands that are not burdens. We love you, Lord. Please help us to show it by living faithfully.

# Known by Actions
## Proverbs 20:11-13

## Memory Verse
*Even a child is known by his actions, by whether his conduct is pure and right (Proverbs 20:11).*

## Attention Grabber
Mention nice things the kids' friends have done, without saying any names. Have the kids tell who you're describing.

## Living It
Jesus said that you can recognize whether or not people are his followers by their fruits, by what they do (Matthew 7:20). That's how people will know if you're a follower of Jesus, too. The best way they can tell is by how you show love to people (John 13:35).

## Discussion Questions
◉ Can most people in the neighborhood and at school tell you're a believer? How?
◉ Do you think most people feel loved when they talk to you? Why or why not?

## Prayer Prompter
Help us to do what's pure and right, so that we show love to the people around us.

# Honest Business
**Proverbs 20:14-30**

### Memory Verse
*"It's no good, it's no good!" says the buyer; then off he goes and boasts about his purchase (Proverbs 20:14).*

### Attention Grabber
Have the kids show you something they have bought or traded to get, such as baseball cards. Ask if they got good deals and if the deals were fair.

### Living It
When we buy things, we need to be careful that as we're trying to get a good deal, we don't take advantage of other people. Some people say, "That's business," as if that is an excuse for treating people badly, but it isn't. We should be as fair in business as we are in all other situations.

### Discussion Questions
ⓓ How can you be sure you are fair when you trade or buy?
ⓓ How can you be sure you are fair when you sell?

### Prayer Prompter
Please help us to be honest and fair in all of our dealings.

# Do Right

## Memory Verse
*To do what is right and just is more acceptable to the Lord than sacrifice (Proverbs 21:3).*

## Attention Grabber
Beforehand, place a gift bow on the top of an empty box. As you begin the devotion, show the kids the box and then show the inside. Explain that religious rituals are hollow gifts to God if we have not given him our hearts.

## Living It
Micah 6:6-8 says that what God wants more than sacrifices is for you "to act justly and to love mercy and to walk humbly with your God." In Mark 12:33, Jesus said that loving God and others was more important than the rituals of the time. The attitude of the heart is what gives meaning to rituals. God prefers that we do what he tells us the first time instead of doing wrong and apologizing afterward. He wants us to avoid the pain that sin causes us, him, and others. When we sin, God does want us to repent and return to him, but he would prefer that we had stayed with him all along.

## Discussion Questions
◎ Have you ever taken your body to church to worship God but left your heart and mind somewhere else? What can you do when you feel that way?
◎ What are some of the rituals of your church? What are they supposed to show about your heart?

## Prayer Prompter
Please help us to act justly, love mercy, and walk humbly with you.

# Get Along
**Proverbs 21:9-12**

## Memory Verse
*Better to live on a corner of the roof than share a house with a quarrelsome wife (Proverbs 21:9).*

## Attention Grabber
No matter what the weather is like, try to have your devotion outdoors. Have the kids look up at the roof of the building where you live. Explain that one of our basic needs is shelter because it can be miserable to be outside for too long; however, it's even more miserable to live inside a house with someone who constantly tries to fight.

## Living It
We wouldn't want to live with a quarrelsome person, so we should try not to be that kind of person ourselves. Right now you can start trying to be the kind of person you might want to marry someday—someone who knows how to get along. And if you do want to marry, you should be careful not to choose someone who wants to argue about everything.

## Discussion Questions
- What can you stop doing that will help our family get along better?
- What can you start doing that will help?

## Prayer Prompter
Please help us learn to get along well with others, and if we marry, help us to marry people who have learned that also.

# The Cry of the Poor
## Proverbs 21:13-22

## Memory Verse

*If a man shuts his ears to the cry of the poor, he too will cry out and not be answered (Proverbs 21:13).*

## Attention Grabber

Try on one another's shoes. Explain that when people say, "Walk a mile in my shoes," they mean that they want you to think about how you would feel in their situation. God wants us to empathize with the poor and help them.

## Living It

God doesn't want us to ignore the needs of the people around us. Sometimes it's easy to pretend that no one around us is suffering, but that isn't true. God wants us to have compassion for the poor and help them. First John 3:17 says, "If anyone has material possessions and sees his brother in need but has no pity on him, how can the love of God be in him?"

## Discussion Questions

◉ If you were in need, how would you want people to help you?
◉ Who do you know with financial problems, and how do you think God wants you to help them?

## Prayer Prompter

Please help us to be sensitive to the needs of the people around us. Please show us how you want us to help.

# Guard Your Mouth

**Proverbs 21:23-28**

## Memory Verse

*He who guards his mouth and his tongue keeps himself from calamity (Proverbs 21:23).*

## Attention Grabber

Have three family members act like the monkeys that see no evil, hear no evil, and speak no evil by having one cover his eyes, one his ears, and one his mouth. Emphasize that the memory verse is about speaking no evil.

## Living It

What does a person mean when he says he "put his foot in his mouth"? (He said the wrong thing.) Sometimes saying the wrong thing might just cause embarrassment, but sometimes it can get people into big trouble! We should be careful about what words we let out of our mouths so that we don't get ourselves into trouble.

## Discussion Questions

- Can you think of a time you put your foot in your mouth? What happened?
- How can you keep from saying the wrong thing?

## Prayer Prompter

Please help us to be careful about what we say.

# God's Side Wins
## Proverbs 21:29-31

### Memory Verse
*There is no wisdom, no insight, no plan that can succeed against the Lord (Proverbs 21:30).*

### Attention Grabber
Wear a T-shirt and cap from your favorite sports team. Emphasize that when you go to a sporting event, you choose which side to support. Explain that there is a much more important decision to make about which side you're on spiritually.

### Living It
Joshua told the Israelites, "Choose for yourselves this day whom you will serve.... But as for me and my household, we will serve the Lord" (Joshua 24:15). Serving the Lord is a smart choice because God's side always wins! Romans 8:37-39 says that "we are more than conquerors through him who loved us," because nothing can "separate us from the love of God that is in Christ Jesus our Lord." Don't be discouraged when it seems like the bad guys are winning. Trust that God will only let things happen that will be good for us in the end (1 Peter 1:6, 7).

### Discussion Questions
- When have you fought against a temptation and won? How did you win?
- Why don't you always see good win over evil right away?

### Prayer Prompter
We are glad to be on your side, Lord! Help us to stay with you.

# A Good Name
## Proverbs 22:1

### Memory Verse

*A good name is more desirable than great riches; to be esteemed is better than silver or gold (Proverbs 22:1).*

### Attention Grabber

If you know the origin of your surname or stories about ancestors in your genealogy, tell the kids. Also, tell them why you chose their first names.

### Living It

When you walk out of your home, you represent more than just yourself. You represent your whole family! People will make judgments about you and the rest of your family based on the way you behave. How you act reveals more about your character than how much money you have or how many possessions you own. You should live with as much integrity and honor as you can so that you can represent yourself, your family, and God well.

### Discussion Questions

◉ What do other people think of your family? Why?
◉ What kind of behaviors could soil your family name? (To parent: emphasize that even if your children ever disappointed you, you would always love them and try to help them.)

### Prayer Prompter

Please help all of us to live in a way that brings honor to you and to our family.

**A Good Name**

# God Made Us All

**Proverbs 22:2-4**

 ### Memory Verse

*Rich and poor have this in common: The Lord is the Maker of them all (Proverbs 22:2).*

 ### Attention Grabber

Come to the devotion wearing shorts. As you slip a baggy pair of pants on over your shorts, ask what this expression means: "We all put our pants on one leg at a time." Explain that all of us have much in common—whether wealthy or poor. We're all human beings.

 ### Living It

People who do not have much money often try to hide that fact as if it is shameful. Sometimes people who have a lot of money try to show it off as if they are better than those who have less. Whether we are rich or poor, we are all of great value to the Creator who made us.

 ### Discussion Questions

- What do the rich and the poor have in common?
- How might you treat people differently if you always thought of them as God's creations?

 ### Prayer Prompter

Thank you for creating and loving all of us.

# Train a Child
**Proverbs 22:5-29**

### Memory Verse
*Train a child in the way he should go, and when he is old he will not turn from it (Proverbs 22:6).*

### Attention Grabber
Have the kids try to part their hair on a different side than usual. Explain that when you first get a haircut, you have to train the hair which way to go. Eventually the hair just naturally falls into place.

### Living It
Parents need to show their children the way God wants them to go. When the children are adults, they will stay on the path, because they can see the wisdom of following God.

### Discussion Questions
◎ Are there things your parents need to train you about more?
◎ In what ways is following God easier for you than it once was?

### Prayer Prompter
Please give parents wisdom in training their children. Help us all to stay on the way we should go.

# Show Restraint

**Proverbs 23:1-4**

### Memory Verse

*Do not wear yourself out to get rich; have the wisdom to show restraint (Proverbs 23:4).*

### Attention Grabber

Draw dollar signs on the lenses of a pair of inexpensive sunglasses with mustard in a squeeze bottle, squeezeable cheese spread, or cake decorating frosting. (Do not use anything abrasive.) Wear the sunglasses as you read the memory verse. Emphasize that some people keep their eyes on money so much that they can't see anything else.

### Living It

It isn't good to sit around being idle (2 Thessalonians 3:7), but we shouldn't go to the other extreme and be so greedy that we work ourselves to death either. It is important to keep our lives balanced.

### Discussion Questions

◉ What do you think people mean by the term "workaholic"?
◉ If people work too much at their jobs, what other parts of their lives can suffer? Why?

### Prayer Prompter

Please help us to be hardworking, but not greedy. Help us keep our priorities in order so that we don't sacrifice what matters more than money.

# Money Sprouts Wings

**Proverbs 23:5-21**

## Memory Verse
*Cast but a glance at riches, and they are gone, for they will surely sprout wings and fly off to the sky like an eagle (Proverbs 23:5).*

## Attention Grabber
Use the directions on page 267 to make a flying dollar bill.

## Living It
It's easier to spend money than earn it, isn't it? What takes days and weeks to earn can be spent in seconds. Don't focus on money and what it buys; focus on God. He'll make sure you have what you need. Matthew 6:32, 33 says, "For the pagans run after all these things, and your heavenly Father knows that you need them. But seek first his kingdom and his righteousness, and all these things will be given to you as well."

## Discussion Questions
◉ Does your money disappear quickly? Why or why not?
◉ Do you think about money a lot? Why or why not?

## Prayer Prompter
Please help us to keep our focus on you rather than money. Give us wisdom about earning, saving, and spending money.

# Honor Mom and Dad
**Proverbs 23:22, 23**

## Memory Verse
*Listen to your father, who gave you life, and do not despise your mother when she is old (Proverbs 23:22).*

## Attention Grabber
Beforehand, find snapshots of Mom and Dad for each child. Have the kids make stand-up photo cutouts using plastic foam plates or cardboard and the directions on page 268.

## Living It
Colossians 3:20 says, "Children, obey your parents in everything, for this pleases the Lord." In Exodus 20:12, one of the Ten Commandments says, "Honor your father and your mother, so that you may live long in the land the Lord your God is giving you." Honoring parents includes listening to their advice and loving them. God wants our relationship with our parents to be close even when we are old.

## Discussion Questions
◎ What advice from your parents has been especially helpful for you?
◎ What could help your relationship with your parents to be stronger?

## Prayer Prompter
Please help us always to have good relationships with our parents.

# Great Joy for Parents
**Proverbs 23:24-35**

## Memory Verse
*The father of a righteous man has great joy; he who has a wise son delights in him (Proverbs 23:24).*

## Attention Grabber
Tell the kids times when it has given you great joy to see that they are right with God and that they have wisdom.

## Living It
It gives parents joy to see their children wisely follow God, because they know this is the way their children will be truly happy. When their children try to be like Jesus, parents can be at peace knowing their children will avoid many of the troubles that the foolish will experience.

## Discussion Questions
◉ Do you feel like you please your parents? Why or why not?
◉ How will following God save both you and your parents grief?

## Prayer Prompter
Please help us to bring our parents joy. Help us to follow you and have wisdom always.

# Avoid Evil

## Memory Verse
*Do not envy wicked men, do not desire their company (Proverbs 24:1).*

## Attention Grabber
Explain that we're influenced by the people that we hang around with. Look at class photos or a class roster together, and ask the kids which kids are a good influence on others. Ask why. Suggest ways they can build friendships with the kids who would be a good influence on them.

## Living It
Sometimes it's tempting to be friends with people who do bad things. They might seem cool or popular. But if they cause us to get into trouble, they won't be good friends for us. God wants us to love everyone and treat everyone well, but our closest friends should be people who will encourage our relationship with God, not discourage it.

## Discussion Questions
◉ Have you ever felt jealous of people who didn't try to obey God? Why or why not?
◉ Why is it important to choose friends who love God?

## Prayer Prompter
Please help us to see clearly the benefits of following you, and help us wisely choose friends who encourage our relationship with you.

# Bounce Back
**Proverbs 24:15, 16**

## Memory Verse
*Though a righteous man falls seven times, he rises again, but the wicked are brought down by calamity (Proverbs 24:16).*

## Attention Grabber
Ask how believers are like basketballs. Drop a basketball and say, "Believers bounce back!"

## Living It
Have you ever played with a jack-in-the-box? No matter how many times the lid comes down on it, the character pops back up again. When the trials of life come down on us like that, God helps us to rise back up, too. A boxer isn't a loser when he gets knocked down; he only loses if he stays down. Everyone gets hit by life's "hard knocks" at times, but we don't have to let things hold us down. When we turn to God, he lifts us back on our feet. He renews our strength and hope. Isaiah 40:31 says, "But those who hope in the Lord will renew their strength. They will soar on wings like eagles; they will run and not grow weary, they walk and not be faint."

## Discussion Questions
◉ What are examples of calamities, or serious troubles, that both believers and nonbelievers may face?
◉ How do people who trust God respond differently to tragedies than those who don't trust God?

## Prayer Prompter
Please remind us to turn to you when we experience calamities, so that we're able to "bounce back" from them.

# Stay Welcome
## Proverbs 24:17–25:17

### Memory Verse
*Seldom set foot in your neighbor's house—too much of you, and he will hate you (Proverbs 25:17).*

### Attention Grabber
Work together with your family to refurbish an old welcome mat by painting it with acrylic paints or attaching decorations with craft glue or a glue gun. Explain that just like a welcome mat can get worn out, we can "wear out our welcome" if we spend too much time at other people's houses.

### Living It
It is fun to go to other people's houses, but while we're there, it's important to be sensitive so that we don't overstay our welcome. We need to make sure that we leave before they get too tired, and we need to be sure we're not taking up too much of their time if they have other things they need to do. Also, it's important to invite them to our house, too. First Peter 4:9 says to "offer hospitality."

### Discussion Questions
- How can you tell if you are overstaying your welcome at someone's home?
- Who would you like to invite for a visit? How could you offer hospitality to them?

### Prayer Prompter
Thank you for our friends and neighbors. Please help us to be sensitive to others.

# Words Can Hurt
**Proverbs 25:18**

### Memory Verse
*Like a club or a sword or a sharp arrow is the man who gives false testimony against his neighbor (Proverbs 25:18).*

### Attention Grabber
Let the kids make arrows out of string cheese (individually packaged mozzarella sticks). Cut a notch on each end of the pieces of cheese. Then have each kid poke the side of a Doritos® tortilla chip into one end of the cheese for the arrowhead. Have each poke the point of a chip into the other end for the feathers.

### Living It
Words can hurt people. What we say about people and to them can hurt their feelings, their reputations, and even their lives. It is important to be careful about what we say, and to tell the truth always.

### Discussion Questions
- Has anyone ever lied about you? How did it make you feel?
- Are little lies OK? Why or why not?

### Prayer Prompter
Please help us to be honest, and to be careful not to say things that could hurt others.

# Be Reliable
## Proverbs 25:19

### Memory Verse
*Like a bad tooth or a lame foot is reliance on the unfaithful in times of trouble (Proverbs 25:19).*

### Attention Grabber
Unscrew a leg off of a table or chair. Show the kids how unstable the piece of furniture is when it doesn't have the support of all its legs.

### Living It
The Bible calls the church one body (Romans 12:5). We need to help each other and support each other like parts of a body do. It is important not to let people down when they need to rely on us.

### Discussion Questions
◉ What kinds of help do other people need from you?
◉ What sacrifices do you think you might have to make to help people in trouble?

### Prayer Prompter
Please help us to be reliable when people need us.

# Be Compassionate
## Proverbs 25:20-26

### Memory Verse

*Like one who takes away a garment on a cold day, or like vinegar poured on soda, is one who sings songs to a heavy heart (Proverbs 25:20).*

### Attention Grabber

Pour baking soda into a bowl so that the baking soda forms a heart shape. Emphasize that when someone's heart is heavy, she feels sad. The person may need sympathy rather than a party. If we act silly around someone sad, we might stir up pain like vinegar stirs up soda. Let the kids add tablespoons of vinegar to the soda.

### Living It

When someone is sad, God wants us to try to understand how she feels. He says to "mourn with those who mourn" (Romans 12:15). It would be insensitive to sing and act silly and crazy around someone who is going through a hard time. Being insensitive is sometimes called being "cold" because it can make someone feel as if her coat were taken away on a wintry day.

### Discussion Questions

- When your friends feel alone and sad, how can you show that you care?
- What have friends done to help you when you have felt bad?

### Prayer Prompter

Please help us to lift our friends' spirits without being insensitive to the pain they feel.

# Too Much Honey
## Proverbs 25:27

### Memory Verse

*It is not good to eat too much honey, nor is it honorable to seek one's own honor (Proverbs 25:27).*

### Attention Grabber

Make chicken nuggets that the kids can dip in honey, or make honey butter (mix 1/2 cup butter with 1/4 cup honey) that they can spread on bread.

### Living It

Sweets taste good, but too much of them are bad for our health (Proverbs 25:16). It is bad for our spiritual health to try to get people to admire and praise us. It is good to do honorable things, but it's not good to try to be noticed for them. Paul said, "We were not looking for praise from men, not from you or anyone else" (1 Thessalonians 2:6). Jesus said, "Be careful not to do your 'acts of righteousness' before men, to be seen by them. If you do, you will have no reward from your Father in heaven" (Matthew 6:1).

### Discussion Questions

◉ How have you felt differently when you did something for God rather than when you did it for people's praise?

◉ Why is God's praise and encouragement better than that of people?

### Prayer Prompter

Please help us to serve with pure motives. Help us to be satisfied with the praise and encouragement you give us, rather than trying to get it from other people.

# Have Self-Control

**Proverbs 25:28–26:11**

## Memory Verse

*Like a city whose walls are broken down is a man who lacks self-control (Proverbs 25:28).*

## Attention Grabber

Let the kids build a miniature wall out of Lego™ plastic construction toys or Tootsie® Roll candy. Explain that in Bible times, a city's walls were its protection from enemies.

## Living It

Having self-control protects us from our enemy, the devil. When he throws temptations toward us, we need to block them the way a city's walls blocked an enemy's arrows. Before people become believers, they are slaves to sin (Romans 6:17). But when they accept Jesus, they have the Holy Spirit to help them control themselves. One of the fruit of the Spirit is self-control (Galatians 5:22, 23). As the line from "Jesus Loves Me" says, "Little ones to him belong. They are weak, but he is strong." If we pray for self-control and trust God for it, he will help us.

## Discussion Questions

◉ In what ways do you have self-control and in what ways do you lack it?

◉ What are ways to increase your self-control?

## Prayer Prompter

Please help us have more self-control.

# Don't Meddle

## Memory Verse

*Like one who seizes a dog by the ears is a passer-by who meddles in a quarrel not his own (Proverbs 26:17).*

## Attention Grabber

Grab a stuffed animal by the ears. Ask the kids what would happen if you did this to a real animal.

## Living It

Just as a dog might bite you if you grab its ears, other people may get mad at you if you stick your nose into their disagreements. It is usually better to let people work out their problems between themselves. Often they will solve their disagreements more quickly if others don't complicate matters. However, there are situations in which people need to get involved, such as to help someone who has been hurt or to defend someone who can't defend herself. In situations in which no one is getting hurt, it's wise to follow the counsel of 1 Thessalonians 4:11 and "mind your own business."

## Discussion Questions

- If you only know one side of a situation, how might your advice about that situation be incorrect?
- How can you be a good listener and show compassion without encouraging people to gossip about disagreements they have had with others?

## Prayer Prompter

Please help us to stay out of petty quarrels that are none of our business.

# Only Joking

**Proverbs 26:18, 19**

## Memory Verse

*Like a madman shooting firebrands or deadly arrows is a man who deceives his neighbor and says, "I was only joking!" (Proverbs 26:18, 19).*

## Attention Grabber

Roast marshmallows on skewers over a barbecue grill. Let one of the marshmallows catch on fire. Explain that it looks a little like a flaming arrow. If you must stay indoors, spear a marshmallow with an old fork, hold it over a baking dish in the kitchen, and light it. After it's flaming, blow it out. (Don't let the kids roast marshmallows indoors.)

## Living It

A madman is someone who acts without thinking in advance about the damage he might cause. A flaming arrow could hurt people, and our jokes can hurt them, too. Just because we say that we're only kidding, doesn't mean that the other person will believe we didn't mean what we said. Also, it's dishonest for us to say we were kidding if we were actually serious. There are several kinds of humor that lift people's spirits rather than hurt them. Be sure to joke only in ways that make everyone feel good.

## Discussion Questions

- How could laughing at someone change the way he feels about himself?
- What kind of jokes hurt, and what kind are good?

## Prayer Prompter

Please help us to joke only in ways that make everyone feel good.

# Without Gossip
## Proverbs 26:20-23

### Memory Verse

*Without wood a fire goes out; without gossip a quarrel dies down (Proverbs 26:20).*

### Attention Grabber

In a barbeque grill outdoors, arrange wooden toothpicks to make a miniature "campfire." Light the fire. Explain that if you kept adding wood, the fire would continue to burn, but if you didn't add any wood, the flames would die out.

### Living It

When people are in a heated argument, it will usually die down eventually. But if people gossip about the argument, that adds fuel to the flames. The people who are already angry have even more reason to be angry. It's good for us to hold our tongues and let tempers cool.

### Discussion Questions

- Why is it tempting to gossip when we're angry?
- When you're trying to forgive, how is it harder if others gossip and say, "You have every right to be mad"?
- Has anyone ever gossiped about you when you were in an argument? What did you do?

### Prayer Prompter

Please help us resist the temptation to gossip. Please help us forgive those who gossip about us.

# What Goes Around ...
**Proverbs 26:24-28**

## Memory Verse
*If a man digs a pit, he will fall into it; if a man rolls a stone, it will roll back on him (Proverbs 26:27).*

## Attention Grabber
If you have one, show the kids a picture or figurine of the Wile E. Coyote™ or Road Runner™ cartoon character. Ask the kids what always happens to the coyote when he tries to harm the roadrunner. Emphasize that if we try to harm others, we may be harmed ourselves.

## Living It
Sometimes when people try to set a trap for others, they get caught in it themselves. That's what happened to Haman, the man who tried to get the king to order the hanging of Mordecai (Queen Esther's father by adoption). Esther 7:10 says, "So they hanged Haman on the gallows he had prepared for Mordecai." Just like the Golden Rule says to do to others what we want them to do to us, we should not do to them what we would not want them to do to us.

## Discussion Questions
- Have you ever tattled on someone and gotten in trouble yourself?
- If you put down others to try to make yourself look better, how might you actually look?

## Prayer Prompter
Please help us to love people so much that we only want good things to happen to them.

# Who Knows the Future?

**Proverbs 27:1-12**

## Memory Verse

*Do not boast about tomorrow, for you do not know what a day may bring forth (Proverbs 27:1).*

## Attention Grabber

Look at an old monthly calendar page together. Circle events you planned to attend but didn't. Emphasize that we have hopes and plans for the future, but we don't know how circumstances will change them. We need to be humble and remember that God's the one who really is in control of our lives.

## Living It

Have you ever been surprised by how differently a day went than you expected? We really don't know what the future holds, and it is prideful to act like we do. James 4:13-16 talks about making plans for the future. James says that we don't know what will happen tomorrow and we "ought to say, 'If it is the Lord's will, we will live and do this or that.'" We should not boast about our plans and act like we know more than we really do.

## Discussion Questions

◎ When have you bragged about something you planned to accomplish before you achieved it? What happened?

◎ How can you be sure the goals you have for yourself are the same as God's plans for you?

## Prayer Prompter

Please help us to stay humble, remembering that you are the one who is in charge of what happens in our lives.

# Iron Sharpens Iron
**Proverbs 27:13-18**

 ### Memory Verse
*As iron sharpens iron, so one man sharpens another (Proverbs 27:17).*

 ### Attention Grabber
If you have a knife sharpener, sharpen a knife and show the kids the metal inside the knife sharpener. Explain that when the metal of a knife sharpener contacts the metal of the knife, it sharpens the knife so the knife can accomplish its purpose.

 ### Living It
Contact with a sharpener helps a knife to be better prepared for a chef's use. Contact with people helps us to be better prepared for God's use. Other people challenge us, encourage us, motivate us, and more. Even Paul, who was very strong in the Lord, wanted to be with other believers because they were "mutually encouraged by each other's faith" (Romans 1:11, 12).

 ### Discussion Questions
- ◉ How do your friends help you to become a better person?
- ◉ What effect do you have on your friends?

 ### Prayer Prompter
Help us to spend time with people who help us to become more fit for your service, and please help us to be a good influence on others.

# Your Heart Reflects You

## Memory Verse

*As water reflects a face, so a man's heart reflects the man (Proverbs 27:19).*

## Attention Grabber

Have everyone look in a mirror. Explain that our reflections in a lake or mirror show our faces, but we have to look deeper than that to see the true condition of our hearts. Our hearts show who we really are.

## Living It

You can see what your face is like by looking at your reflection, but that won't show you your true self. You can see what your character is like by looking into your heart and by listening to what comes out of it. Luke 6:45 says, "The good man brings good things out of the good stored up in his heart, and the evil man brings evil things out of the evil stored up in his heart. For out of the overflow of his heart his mouth speaks."

## Discussion Questions

- How can you get rid of what shouldn't be in your heart?
- Have you invited Jesus into every part of your heart? (If your child seems ready to trust Jesus, see page 270 for help.)

## Prayer Prompter

Please help us to see ourselves the way we truly are. Please cleanse every part of our hearts.

# Tested by Praise

**Proverbs 27:21-27**

## Memory Verse

*The crucible for silver and the furnace for gold, but man is tested by the praise he receives (Proverbs 27:21).*

## Attention Grabber

Beforehand, blow up a balloon, but don't tie it. Draw a face on it, and let out the air. During the devotion, praise the balloon as if it is a person. Blow into the balloon after each compliment. Emphasize that it's hard not to get a "big head" when we receive a lot of praise.

## Living It

When you have heard an audience clap for a Christian singer, have you ever seen the singer point upward? It's as if the singer is saying, "Clap for God, not me." When we receive praise, it can tempt us to become proud. Instead of receiving the glory ourselves, we need to give it to God for enabling us to do whatever is being praised.

## Discussion Questions

◉ What are ways to praise God when others try to give you credit for what he has done through you?

◉ How can enjoying praise too much change your motives from pure to impure?

## Prayer Prompter

We praise you for all you do through us, Lord. Help us to remain humble, always aware of how much we need you.

# Running Scared
**Proverbs 28:1-10**

## Memory Verse

*The wicked man flees though no one pursues, but the righteous are as bold as a lion (Proverbs 28:1).*

## Attention Grabber

Have the kids take turns imitating the way a criminal might look over his shoulder to see if he's being followed.

## Living It

Sin has consequences, one of which is getting caught. People who sin can't be at peace, because they're always on the lookout for when the consequences of their actions will catch up with them. If we're right with God, we have nothing to fear. The Bible mentions the boldness of some Christians. Joseph of Arimathea went boldly to Pilate and asked for Jesus' body (Mark 15:43) so he could place it in his own tomb. Paul and Barnabas spoke boldly for the Lord (Acts 14:3). Apollos spoke boldly about Jesus in the Jewish synagogue (Acts 18:24-26). All of us can "come boldly unto the throne of grace, that we may obtain mercy, and find grace to help in time of need" (Hebrews 4:16, *KJV*).

## Discussion Questions

- In what situations is it good to be bold?
- What do nonbelievers have to worry about that believers don't worry about?

## Prayer Prompter

Thank you for the peace you give to us and the boldness to stand up for what is right without being afraid.

**Running Scared**

247

# Wealthy and Wise?

**Proverbs 28:11, 12**

---

## Memory Verse

*A rich man may be wise in his own eyes, but a poor man who has discernment sees through him (Proverbs 28:11).*

## Attention Grabber

Begin quoting part of Benjamin Franklin's rhyme and see if the kids can finish it: "Early to bed and early to rise, . . ." ("makes a man healthy, wealthy, and wise"). Ask, "Are the wealthy always wise?"

## Living It

As a person gains money, he doesn't necessarily gain wisdom. Pride often comes with wealth. Romans 12:3 warns, "Do not think of yourself more highly than you ought, but rather think of yourself with sober judgment." It's more important to be discerning than it is to have money. Philippians 1:9, 10 says, "And this is my prayer: that your love may abound more and more in knowledge and depth of insight, so that you may be able to discern what is best and may be pure and blameless until the day of Christ."

## Discussion Questions

◉ Do you know things about people that they don't realize about themselves? Is it likely that others know things about you that you might not realize?

◉ What's the difference between being discerning and being judgmental? (*Discerning:* able to see a situation accurately, especially what's right and wrong. *Judgmental:* labeling a person, looking down on her, and doubting she can change.)

## Prayer Prompter

Please help us not to be prideful. Help us to see ourselves and others accurately, and feel love in spite of the flaws we see.

# Don't Hide Sin
**Proverbs 28:13-28**

### Memory Verse
*He who conceals his sins does not prosper, but whoever confesses and renounces them finds mercy (Proverbs 28:13).*

### Attention Grabber
Place a toy arrow or stick under your arm as if you've been shot and say, "They got me!" Ask the kids why it would be unwise to walk around with an arrow in your side. (If you kept ignoring your injury, it would kill you.)

### Living It
Just as we couldn't ignore a serious injury and hope that it would just go away, we can't ignore our sins and hope they will just vanish. We need to confess them to God and give them up. He promises in 1 John 1:9, "If we confess our sins, he is faithful and just and will forgive us our sins and purify us from all unrighteousness."

### Discussion Questions
◉ Why does God want you to repent?
◉ What does it feel like to have your guilt lifted?

### Prayer Prompter
Thank you for being so merciful to us that you are willing to forgive whatever we confess to you. Help us admit our sins to you.

# Control Anger
**Proverbs 29:1-11**

### Memory Verse
*A fool gives full vent to his anger, but a wise man keeps himself under control (Proverbs 29:11).*

### Attention Grabber
Boil water in a pot. Cover the pot with a lid. Have the kids stand back, and direct the steam away from them as you lift the lid slightly to show how the steam escapes.

### Living It
Sometimes being angry is called "being steamed" or "hot under the collar." When we feel angry, holding the anger inside can cause depression or stress. But "flipping our lid," losing our tempers and taking it out on others, can harm people the way steam can hurt them. If you lift the lid of a pot of boiling water, you have to be careful to release the steam away from yourself and others. We need to control our anger, releasing it in ways that don't harm others or ourselves.

### Discussion Questions
- How does it make you feel when others take out their anger on you?
- What helps you to control the way you release your anger?

### Prayer Prompter
Please help us to control our anger and release it in ways that don't harm others.

**Control Anger**

# Kids Need Parents
## Proverbs 29:12-15

### Memory Verse

*The rod of correction imparts wisdom, but a child left to himself disgraces his mother (Proverbs 29:15).*

### Attention Grabber

Have everyone try to do a Tarzan call. Ask the kids if they have ever thought it would be fun to be raised in a jungle like Tarzan or to live alone on a deserted island. Ask how their houses would look, how they would dress, and how they would behave.

### Living It

God gives kids parents and guardians because he knows kids need them! We try to stay involved in your life because we love you and want to help you learn right from wrong. When we discipline you, it's so that you will learn wisdom. Then you will be able to make wise choices as an adult.

### Discussion Questions

◎ How would you like for your parents to be more involved in your life?

◎ What choices would you be able to make better now than you would have been able to make two or three years ago?

### Prayer Prompter

Please help us to listen to our parents and help them to stay involved in our lives. Help us to learn from discipline and to continue to grow in wisdom.

# No Fear

**Proverbs 29:16-25**

## Memory Verse

*Fear of man will prove to be a snare, but whoever trusts in the Lord is kept safe (Proverbs 29:25).*

## Attention Grabber

Make your hands tremble as you ask the kids, "Have you ever been so nervous that your hands shook or your palms got clammy? Why?"

## Living It

Sometimes people are afraid to tell others about Jesus. That fear doesn't come from God. Second Timothy 1:7, 8 *(KJV)* says, "For God hath not given us the spirit of fear; but of power, and of love, and of a sound mind. Be not therefore ashamed of the testimony of our Lord." You may be afraid to speak openly to someone about Jesus because you fear the person might not like you anymore. Galatians 1:10 says, "Am I now trying to win the approval of men, or of God? Or am I trying to please men? If I were still trying to please men, I would not be a servant of Christ."

## Discussion Questions

- If you weren't a Christian, and someone told you about Jesus, would you stop liking that person or would you be grateful for hearing the message? Why?
- How does God help you overcome your fears? How can he help you not be nervous about telling others about him?

## Prayer Prompter

Please help us to overcome our fears, Lord. Especially help us to tell others bravely about you.

# God Gives Justice

**Proverbs 29:26, 27**

## Memory Verse

*Many seek an audience with a ruler, but it is from the Lord that man gets justice (Proverbs 29:26).*

## Attention Grabber

While holding an envelope in your hand, ask, "If this were an invitation for you to visit the White House, how would you feel? Why?"

## Living It

When we need help getting justice, instead of turning to powerful leaders, we should turn to our powerful God. Remember Psalm 121:2, which says, "My help comes from the Lord, the Maker of heaven and earth." Jesus said, "And will not God bring about justice for his chosen ones, who cry out to him day and night? Will he keep putting them off? I tell you, he will see that they get justice, and quickly" (Luke 18:7, 8). Romans 12:19, 20 says that when we need justice, we should "not take revenge, my friends, but leave room for God's wrath, for it is written: 'It is mine to avenge; I will repay,' says the Lord." The Bible goes on to say that instead, we should treat our enemies well by giving them food and drink when they need some. Romans 12:21 says, "Do not be overcome by evil, but overcome evil with good."

## Discussion Questions

- ◉ What are ways that God provides justice?
- ◉ How can you "overcome evil with good"?

## Prayer Prompter

Please help us to forgive others and to trust you for justice.

# Don't Annoy
## Proverbs 30

### Memory Verse

*"For as churning the milk produces butter, and as twisting the nose produces blood, so stirring up anger produces strife"* (Proverbs 30:33).

### Attention Grabber

Pour chilled cream into a small jar until the jar is half full. Put the lid on the jar tightly. Let the kids take turns shaking the jar up and down for several minutes until chunks of butter form. Salt the butter to taste and spread the butter on crackers.

### Living It

Have you ever seen people try to get the stone-faced Buckingham Palace guards to smile or get angry? In a similar way, sometimes people try to annoy others to get them to lose their tempers. That leads to fighting as surely as churning or shaking cream forms butter. God wants us to be peacemakers (Matthew 5:9). Romans 12:18 says, "If it is possible, as far as it depends on you, live at peace with everyone."

### Discussion Questions

- What are some ways kids behave that annoy other kids and adults?
- How can you tell when someone is getting annoyed by what you are saying or doing? What can you do to avoid annoying others?

### Prayer Prompter

Please help us not to annoy others.

# Far More Than Rubies

**Proverbs 31:1-28**

## Memory Verse

*A wife of noble character who can find? She is worth far more than rubies (Proverbs 31:10).*

## Attention Grabber

Make cherry gelatin using the recipe on the side of the box. Cut the red gelatin into gem-shaped "rubies" and give one to each family member.

## Living It

The Bible's description of a virtuous woman emphasizes the value of a wise woman, and it gives guidelines about how women can serve their families and communities. In fact, the example of this woman in Proverbs would be a good example for anyone to try to follow. Let's list some of the characteristics of "a wife of noble character" mentioned in the verses of Proverbs 31.

## Discussion Questions

- Did any of the characteristics of the wife of noble character surprise you? If so, which?
- Which line was your favorite? Why?

## Prayer Prompter

Please help everyone in our family to develop noble character and, if we choose to marry, to marry others who have developed noble character as well.

# A Woman to Be Praised
**Proverbs 31:29-31**

### Memory Verse
*Charm is deceptive, and beauty is fleeting; but a woman who fears the Lord is to be praised (Proverbs 31:30).*

### Attention Grabber
Make family members look elderly by putting talcum powder in their hair and drawing wrinkles with an eyebrow pencil or eyeliner.

### Living It
A person might choose who he will marry based on a charming personality or attractiveness. But charm can hide the true nature of a person. And people will grow older and lose their youthful beauty eventually. Instead, a person should choose a spouse who respects and loves God. That's what's most important.

### Discussion Questions
◎ Why shouldn't you marry someone just because the person is attractive and has a charming personality?
◎ What is the most important quality in a spouse?

### Prayer Prompter
Please help us to be people who love and respect you, Lord. And if we choose to marry, help us to make wise decisions about who to marry.

# Optional Supplies

Most of the devotions use items you probably already have. If you don't happen to have the needed materials, don't worry. There is usually a simple alternate activity. If you would like to plan ahead to be sure you have everything, please make yourself a shopping list by circling the items you need to buy. If a devotion isn't listed, no materials are needed for it.

page 17    celery, jar of water, red or blue food coloring; or plant clippings, jar(s) of water
page 18    paper plates, duct tape, markers or crayons, scrap paper
page 21    paper, pens
page 23    apples, knife, tempera paint, paper
page 24    black paper and colored chalk or white paper and markers
page 26    pens, photocopies of My Week from page 264 or plain paper
page 27    silver item such as jewelry; or silver dinnerware, polish, soft cloths
page 28    alarm clock
page 31    bed linens
page 33    colored chalk, blue construction paper
page 34    paper, pencils
page 35    protective gear such as a helmet, a shield (trash can lid), knee and elbow pads, bug spray
page 36    construction paper or photocopies of family tree from page 265, markers, scissors, reprints of family photos, glue, picture frames
page 37    Tootsie® Roll candy or taffy
page 38    blanket, picnic food and supplies
page 40    sand timer; or salt, paper, jar
page 41    cups, bowls, beverage
page 42    binoculars or paper cups
page 43    clothing and accessories to dress like a rebellious teen
page 44    mousetraps, magnets, glue; or box, stick, string
page 46    box of tissues covered with gift wrap or fabric, index cards, pens, glue
page 48    chalk (white or colored), water
page 50    paper, pen, Bible
page 51    calendar, pen
page 52    paper and pencils, crayons, or markers
page 53    knife, toasted English muffins with tomato sauce, shredded cheese, black olives, pepperoni; or with marmalade, raisins, pretzel sticks
page 54    glow-in-the-dark object
page 55    paper plates, banana pudding or vanilla pudding with yellow food coloring
page 56    sealable plastic bags, shelled peanuts, spoon or hammer, knife, crackers; or hard-boiled eggs still in shells
page 57    unpopped popcorn, popcorn popper or pot
page 58    can(s) of white shaving cream, water for rinsing
page 59    paper, markers
page 60    bell, horn, or flag
page 61    jar, permanent markers or paint pens
page 62    note cards, pens, envelopes
page 64    recipe and ingredients for slime from page 269
page 65    folders, decorating materials (markers, stickers, ribbons, etc.)
page 66    camera with film inside

# Know-It-By-Heart

## Chart for _____

| | | | | |
|---|---|---|---|---|
| ❑ Psalm 1:3 | ❑ Psalm 40:5 | ❑ Psalm 118:24 | ❑ Proverbs 10:9 | ❑ Proverbs 19:2 |
| ❑ Psalm 3:3 | ❑ Psalm 40:8 | ❑ Psalm 119:11 | ❑ Proverbs 10:12 | ❑ Proverbs 19:3 |
| ❑ Psalm 4:4 | ❑ Psalm 40:10 | ❑ Psalm 119:24 | ❑ Proverbs 10:17 | ❑ Proverbs 19:17 |
| ❑ Psalm 4:8 | ❑ Psalm 42:1 | ❑ Psalm 119:37 | ❑ Proverbs 10:19 | ❑ Proverbs 19:18 |
| ❑ Psalm 5:4 | ❑ Psalm 42:11 | ❑ Psalm 119:73 | ❑ Proverbs 10:25 | ❑ Proverbs 19:20 |
| ❑ Psalm 8:1 | ❑ Psalm 46:10 | ❑ Psalm 119:105 | ❑ Proverbs 11:6 | ❑ Proverbs 20:1 |
| ❑ Psalm 8:3, 4 | ❑ Psalm 47:1 | ❑ Psalm 119:112 | ❑ Proverbs 11:12 | ❑ Proverbs 20:3 |
| ❑ Psalm 9:1 | ❑ Psalm 49:16, 17 | ❑ Psalm 121:2 | ❑ Proverbs 11:13 | ❑ Proverbs 20:6 |
| ❑ Psalm 9:9 | ❑ Psalm 50:10 | ❑ Psalm 127:1 | ❑ Proverbs 11:16 | ❑ Proverbs 20:11 |
| ❑ Psalm 10:4 | ❑ Psalm 51:10 | ❑ Psalm 127:3 | ❑ Proverbs 11:17 | ❑ Proverbs 20:14 |
| ❑ Psalm 12:6 | ❑ Psalm 51:12 | ❑ Psalm 130:3, 4 | ❑ Proverbs 11:22 | ❑ Proverbs 21:3 |
| ❑ Psalm 13:5 | ❑ Psalm 53:2 | ❑ Psalm 133:1 | ❑ Proverbs 11:25 | ❑ Proverbs 21:9 |
| ❑ Psalm 14:1 | ❑ Psalm 55:17 | ❑ Psalm 136:26 | ❑ Proverbs 11:28 | ❑ Proverbs 21:13 |
| ❑ Psalm 16:7 | ❑ Psalm 55:22 | ❑ Psalm 139:1 | ❑ Proverbs 12:1 | ❑ Proverbs 21:23 |
| ❑ Psalm 18:2 | ❑ Psalm 56:3 | ❑ Psalm 139:8 | ❑ Proverbs 12:4 | ❑ Proverbs 21:30 |
| ❑ Psalm 18:25 | ❑ Psalm 56:8 | ❑ Psalm 139:13 | ❑ Proverbs 12:9 | ❑ Proverbs 22:1 |
| ❑ Psalm 19:1 | ❑ Psalm 56:11 | ❑ Psalm 139:14 | ❑ Proverbs 12:10 | ❑ Proverbs 22:2 |
| ❑ Psalm 19:14 | ❑ Psalm 63:8 | ❑ Psalm 139:23, 24 | ❑ Proverbs 12:14 | ❑ Proverbs 22:6 |
| ❑ Psalm 20:7 | ❑ Psalm 66:5 | ❑ Psalm 141:3 | ❑ Proverbs 12:15 | ❑ Proverbs 23:4 |
| ❑ Psalm 22:4 | ❑ Psalm 67:1 | ❑ Psalm 145:2 | ❑ Proverbs 12:16 | ❑ Proverbs 23:5 |
| ❑ Psalm 23:1 | ❑ Psalm 68:5 | ❑ Psalm 145:8 | ❑ Proverbs 12:18 | ❑ Proverbs 23:22 |
| ❑ Psalm 23:2, 3 | ❑ Psalm 68:19 | ❑ Psalm 147:1 | ❑ Proverbs 12:25 | ❑ Proverbs 23:24 |
| ❑ Psalm 23:3 | ❑ Psalm 69:1 | ❑ Psalm 149:4 | ❑ Proverbs 13:20 | ❑ Proverbs 24:1 |
| ❑ Psalm 23:4 | ❑ Psalm 69:30, 31 | ❑ Psalm 150:6 | ❑ Proverbs 13:24 | ❑ Proverbs 24:16 |
| ❑ Psalm 23:5 | ❑ Psalm 71:5 | ❑ Proverbs 1:7 | ❑ Proverbs 14:1 | ❑ Proverbs 25:17 |
| ❑ Psalm 23:6 | ❑ Psalm 71:15 | ❑ Proverbs 1:8 | ❑ Proverbs 14:9 | ❑ Proverbs 25:18 |
| ❑ Psalm 25:7 | ❑ Psalm 72:1 | ❑ Proverbs 1:10 | ❑ Proverbs 14:12 | ❑ Proverbs 25:19 |
| ❑ Psalm 25:15 | ❑ Psalm 73:23 | ❑ Proverbs 2:6 | ❑ Proverbs 14:15 | ❑ Proverbs 25:20 |
| ❑ Psalm 27:1 | ❑ Psalm 74:16 | ❑ Proverbs 2:12, 13 | ❑ Proverbs 14:21 | ❑ Proverbs 25:27 |
| ❑ Psalm 30:5 | ❑ Psalm 77:11 | ❑ Proverbs 3:3 | ❑ Proverbs 14:23 | ❑ Proverbs 25:28 |
| ❑ Psalm 31:7 | ❑ Psalm 84:10 | ❑ Proverbs 3:5, 6 | ❑ Proverbs 14:30 | ❑ Proverbs 26:17 |
| ❑ Psalm 32:2 | ❑ Psalm 86:5 | ❑ Proverbs 3:12 | ❑ Proverbs 15:1 | ❑ Proverbs 26:18, 19 |
| ❑ Psalm 32:9 | ❑ Psalm 86:11 | ❑ Proverbs 3:13-15 | ❑ Proverbs 15:16 | ❑ Proverbs 26:20 |
| ❑ Psalm 33:4 | ❑ Psalm 89:2 | ❑ Proverbs 3:27, 28 | ❑ Proverbs 15:17 | ❑ Proverbs 26:27 |
| ❑ Psalm 33:11 | ❑ Psalm 89:9 | ❑ Proverbs 3:31 | ❑ Proverbs 15:18 | ❑ Proverbs 27:1 |
| ❑ Psalm 33:13, 14 | ❑ Psalm 90:14 | ❑ Proverbs 4:18 | ❑ Proverbs 15:22 | ❑ Proverbs 27:17 |
| ❑ Psalm 34:4 | ❑ Psalm 91:11 | ❑ Proverbs 4:23 | ❑ Proverbs 15:23 | ❑ Proverbs 27:19 |
| ❑ Psalm 34:5 | ❑ Psalm 91:14 | ❑ Proverbs 4:24 | ❑ Proverbs 16:2 | ❑ Proverbs 27:21 |
| ❑ Psalm 34:10 | ❑ Psalm 92:1 | ❑ Proverbs 5:18 | ❑ Proverbs 16:3 | ❑ Proverbs 28:1 |
| ❑ Psalm 34:18 | ❑ Psalm 94:9 | ❑ Proverbs 5:22 | ❑ Proverbs 16:18 | ❑ Proverbs 28:11 |
| ❑ Psalm 34:19 | ❑ Psalm 100:2 | ❑ Proverbs 6:6 | ❑ Proverbs 16:24 | ❑ Proverbs 28:13 |
| ❑ Psalm 36:5 | ❑ Psalm 100:4 | ❑ Proverbs 6:10, 11 | ❑ Proverbs 17:3 | ❑ Proverbs 29:11 |
| ❑ Psalm 37:4 | ❑ Psalm 103:2 | ❑ Proverbs 6:16-19 | ❑ Proverbs 17:22 | ❑ Proverbs 29:15 |
| ❑ Psalm 37:7 | ❑ Psalm 103:12 | ❑ Proverbs 6:27-29 | ❑ Proverbs 17:28 | ❑ Proverbs 29:25 |
| ❑ Psalm 37:21 | ❑ Psalm 112:7 | ❑ Proverbs 9:8 | ❑ Proverbs 18:8 | ❑ Proverbs 29:26 |
| ❑ Psalm 37:37 | ❑ Psalm 116:8 | ❑ Proverbs 10:1 | ❑ Proverbs 18:10 | ❑ Proverbs 30:33 |
| ❑ Psalm 40:1 | ❑ Psalm 118:8 | ❑ Proverbs 10:4 | ❑ Proverbs 18:22 | ❑ Proverbs 31:10 |
| ❑ Psalm 40:2 | ❑ Psalm 118:22 | ❑ Proverbs 10:7 | ❑ Proverbs 18:24 | ❑ Proverbs 31:30 |

# Know-It-By-Heart
## Chart for _____

| | | | | |
|---|---|---|---|---|
| ❏ Psalm 1:3 | ❏ Psalm 40:5 | ❏ Psalm 118:24 | ❏ Proverbs 10:9 | ❏ Proverbs 19:2 |
| ❏ Psalm 3:3 | ❏ Psalm 40:8 | ❏ Psalm 119:11 | ❏ Proverbs 10:12 | ❏ Proverbs 19:3 |
| ❏ Psalm 4:4 | ❏ Psalm 40:10 | ❏ Psalm 119:24 | ❏ Proverbs 10:17 | ❏ Proverbs 19:17 |
| ❏ Psalm 4:8 | ❏ Psalm 42:1 | ❏ Psalm 119:37 | ❏ Proverbs 10:19 | ❏ Proverbs 19:18 |
| ❏ Psalm 5:4 | ❏ Psalm 42:11 | ❏ Psalm 119:73 | ❏ Proverbs 10:25 | ❏ Proverbs 19:20 |
| ❏ Psalm 8:1 | ❏ Psalm 46:10 | ❏ Psalm 119:105 | ❏ Proverbs 11:6 | ❏ Proverbs 20:1 |
| ❏ Psalm 8:3, 4 | ❏ Psalm 47:1 | ❏ Psalm 119:112 | ❏ Proverbs 11:12 | ❏ Proverbs 20:3 |
| ❏ Psalm 9:1 | ❏ Psalm 49:16, 17 | ❏ Psalm 121:2 | ❏ Proverbs 11:13 | ❏ Proverbs 20:6 |
| ❏ Psalm 9:9 | ❏ Psalm 50:10 | ❏ Psalm 127:1 | ❏ Proverbs 11:16 | ❏ Proverbs 20:11 |
| ❏ Psalm 10:4 | ❏ Psalm 51:10 | ❏ Psalm 127:3 | ❏ Proverbs 11:17 | ❏ Proverbs 20:14 |
| ❏ Psalm 12:6 | ❏ Psalm 51:12 | ❏ Psalm 130:3, 4 | ❏ Proverbs 11:22 | ❏ Proverbs 21:3 |
| ❏ Psalm 13:5 | ❏ Psalm 53:2 | ❏ Psalm 133:1 | ❏ Proverbs 11:25 | ❏ Proverbs 21:9 |
| ❏ Psalm 14:1 | ❏ Psalm 55:17 | ❏ Psalm 136:26 | ❏ Proverbs 11:28 | ❏ Proverbs 21:13 |
| ❏ Psalm 16:7 | ❏ Psalm 55:22 | ❏ Psalm 139:1 | ❏ Proverbs 12:1 | ❏ Proverbs 21:23 |
| ❏ Psalm 18:2 | ❏ Psalm 56:3 | ❏ Psalm 139:8 | ❏ Proverbs 12:4 | ❏ Proverbs 21:30 |
| ❏ Psalm 18:25 | ❏ Psalm 56:8 | ❏ Psalm 139:13 | ❏ Proverbs 12:9 | ❏ Proverbs 22:1 |
| ❏ Psalm 19:1 | ❏ Psalm 56:11 | ❏ Psalm 139:14 | ❏ Proverbs 12:10 | ❏ Proverbs 22:2 |
| ❏ Psalm 19:14 | ❏ Psalm 63:8 | ❏ Psalm 139:23, 24 | ❏ Proverbs 12:14 | ❏ Proverbs 22:6 |
| ❏ Psalm 20:7 | ❏ Psalm 66:5 | ❏ Psalm 141:3 | ❏ Proverbs 12:15 | ❏ Proverbs 23:4 |
| ❏ Psalm 22:4 | ❏ Psalm 67:1 | ❏ Psalm 145:2 | ❏ Proverbs 12:16 | ❏ Proverbs 23:5 |
| ❏ Psalm 23:1 | ❏ Psalm 68:5 | ❏ Psalm 145:8 | ❏ Proverbs 12:18 | ❏ Proverbs 23:22 |
| ❏ Psalm 23:2, 3 | ❏ Psalm 68:19 | ❏ Psalm 147:1 | ❏ Proverbs 12:25 | ❏ Proverbs 23:24 |
| ❏ Psalm 23:3 | ❏ Psalm 69:1 | ❏ Psalm 149:4 | ❏ Proverbs 13:20 | ❏ Proverbs 24:1 |
| ❏ Psalm 23:4 | ❏ Psalm 69:30, 31 | ❏ Psalm 150:6 | ❏ Proverbs 13:24 | ❏ Proverbs 24:16 |
| ❏ Psalm 23:5 | ❏ Psalm 71:5 | ❏ Proverbs 1:7 | ❏ Proverbs 14:1 | ❏ Proverbs 25:17 |
| ❏ Psalm 23:6 | ❏ Psalm 71:15 | ❏ Proverbs 1:8 | ❏ Proverbs 14:9 | ❏ Proverbs 25:18 |
| ❏ Psalm 25:7 | ❏ Psalm 72:1 | ❏ Proverbs 1:10 | ❏ Proverbs 14:12 | ❏ Proverbs 25:19 |
| ❏ Psalm 25:15 | ❏ Psalm 73:23 | ❏ Proverbs 2:6 | ❏ Proverbs 14:15 | ❏ Proverbs 25:20 |
| ❏ Psalm 27:1 | ❏ Psalm 74:16 | ❏ Proverbs 2:12, 13 | ❏ Proverbs 14:21 | ❏ Proverbs 25:27 |
| ❏ Psalm 30:5 | ❏ Psalm 77:11 | ❏ Proverbs 3:3 | ❏ Proverbs 14:23 | ❏ Proverbs 25:28 |
| ❏ Psalm 31:7 | ❏ Psalm 84:10 | ❏ Proverbs 3:5, 6 | ❏ Proverbs 14:30 | ❏ Proverbs 26:17 |
| ❏ Psalm 32:2 | ❏ Psalm 86:5 | ❏ Proverbs 3:12 | ❏ Proverbs 15:1 | ❏ Proverbs 26:18, 19 |
| ❏ Psalm 32:9 | ❏ Psalm 86:11 | ❏ Proverbs 3:13-15 | ❏ Proverbs 15:16 | ❏ Proverbs 26:20 |
| ❏ Psalm 33:4 | ❏ Psalm 89:2 | ❏ Proverbs 3:27, 28 | ❏ Proverbs 15:17 | ❏ Proverbs 26:27 |
| ❏ Psalm 33:11 | ❏ Psalm 89:9 | ❏ Proverbs 3:31 | ❏ Proverbs 15:18 | ❏ Proverbs 27:1 |
| ❏ Psalm 33:13, 14 | ❏ Psalm 90:14 | ❏ Proverbs 4:18 | ❏ Proverbs 15:22 | ❏ Proverbs 27:17 |
| ❏ Psalm 34:4 | ❏ Psalm 91:11 | ❏ Proverbs 4:23 | ❏ Proverbs 15:23 | ❏ Proverbs 27:19 |
| ❏ Psalm 34:5 | ❏ Psalm 91:14 | ❏ Proverbs 4:24 | ❏ Proverbs 16:2 | ❏ Proverbs 27:21 |
| ❏ Psalm 34:10 | ❏ Psalm 92:1 | ❏ Proverbs 5:18 | ❏ Proverbs 16:3 | ❏ Proverbs 28:1 |
| ❏ Psalm 34:18 | ❏ Psalm 94:9 | ❏ Proverbs 5:22 | ❏ Proverbs 16:18 | ❏ Proverbs 28:11 |
| ❏ Psalm 34:19 | ❏ Psalm 100:2 | ❏ Proverbs 6:6 | ❏ Proverbs 16:24 | ❏ Proverbs 28:13 |
| ❏ Psalm 36:5 | ❏ Psalm 100:4 | ❏ Proverbs 6:10, 11 | ❏ Proverbs 17:3 | ❏ Proverbs 29:11 |
| ❏ Psalm 37:4 | ❏ Psalm 103:2 | ❏ Proverbs 6:16-19 | ❏ Proverbs 17:22 | ❏ Proverbs 29:15 |
| ❏ Psalm 37:7 | ❏ Psalm 103:12 | ❏ Proverbs 6:27-29 | ❏ Proverbs 17:28 | ❏ Proverbs 29:25 |
| ❏ Psalm 37:21 | ❏ Psalm 112:7 | ❏ Proverbs 9:8 | ❏ Proverbs 18:8 | ❏ Proverbs 29:26 |
| ❏ Psalm 37:37 | ❏ Psalm 116:8 | ❏ Proverbs 10:1 | ❏ Proverbs 18:10 | ❏ Proverbs 30:33 |
| ❏ Psalm 40:1 | ❏ Psalm 118:8 | ❏ Proverbs 10:4 | ❏ Proverbs 18:22 | ❏ Proverbs 31:10 |
| ❏ Psalm 40:2 | ❏ Psalm 118:22 | ❏ Proverbs 10:7 | ❏ Proverbs 18:24 | ❏ Proverbs 31:30 |

# Patterns and Crafts

## Make Music (page 103) and Ways to Praise (page 136)
**Directions for homemade musical instruments:**

 Jingle Bracelet—Thread a chenille stem or string through small sleigh bells. Twist or tie the ends together.

Castanets—Make two loops with tape and place each loop on the top of a clean lid from a frozen juice can. Put your thumb in one loop and your index finger in the other loop. Tap the lids together.

 Drum—Using two pencils or wooden spoons, tap on the lid of an empty container of oats or the plastic lid of an empty coffee can.

Water Xylophone—Fill drinking glasses or jars with water to different levels (add food coloring for fun). Tap the glasses with a metal spoon.

 Shakers—Partially fill empty 35 mm film containers with rice. Put lids on tightly and shake the containers.

Comb Kazoo—Wrap wax paper around a comb and hum into the covered teeth.

Drinking Straw Flute—Blow across the opening of a straw while holding the other end firmly. With your other hand, pinch the straw and slide your fingers up and down the straw to produce different sounds as you blow across the top.

# Room for God (page 26)
## My Week chart

# MY WEEK

| | Sunday | Monday | Tuesday | Wednesday | Thursday | Friday | Saturday |
|---|---|---|---|---|---|---|---|
| 6–7 A.M. | | | | | | | |
| 7–8 A.M. | | | | | | | |
| 8–9 A.M. | | | | | | | |
| 9–10 A.M. | | | | | | | |
| 10–11 A.M. | | | | | | | |
| 11–noon | | | | | | | |
| noon–1 P.M. | | | | | | | |
| 1–2 P.M. | | | | | | | |
| 2–3 P.M. | | | | | | | |
| 3–4 P.M. | | | | | | | |
| 4–5 P.M. | | | | | | | |
| 5–6 P.M. | | | | | | | |
| 6–7 P.M. | | | | | | | |
| 7–8 P.M. | | | | | | | |
| 8–9 P.M. | | | | | | | |
| 9–10 P.M. | | | | | | | |
| 10–11 P.M. | | | | | | | |

# Family Faith (page 36)
**Pattern for family tree**

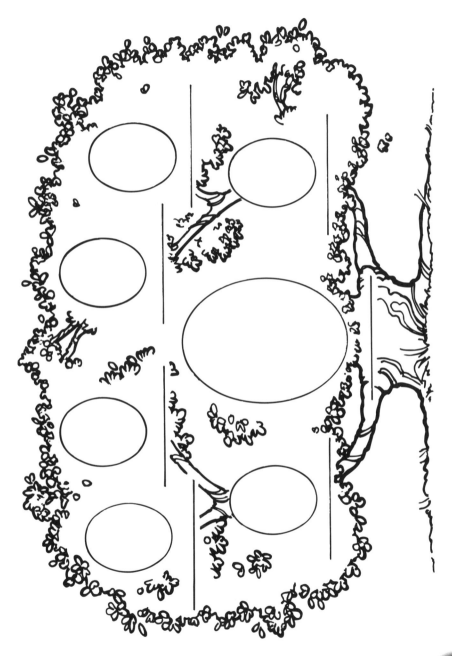

# Praise Every Day (page 132)
**30 Days of Praise chart**

## 30 Days of Praise

# Unless God Builds It (page 121)

**Diagram of house of cards**

# Money Sprouts Wings (page 228)

**Pattern for dollar bill glider:**

Use this pattern to cut "wings" out of a plastic foam plate. Tightly roll a dollar bill lengthwise and flatten it. Poke the rolled, flattened dollar through the slit in the center of the wings.

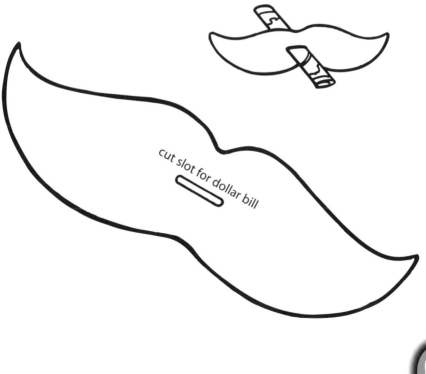

cut slot for dollar bill

# Honor Mom and Dad (page 229)

## Directions for stand-up photo cutouts:

1. Place a snapshot of Mom or Dad on a plastic foam plate or cardboard. Hold both items together firmly.

2. Cut off the background of the picture, cutting through both the photo and the plastic foam or cardboard backing at the same time.

3. Glue the photo cutout and the cutout backing together.

4. For each picture, cut two 1 ½" x 1" strips for a picture stand. In the middle of a long side of each strip, cut a ½" slit.

5. Push the photo cutout into the slits of the two strips so the picture can stand upright.

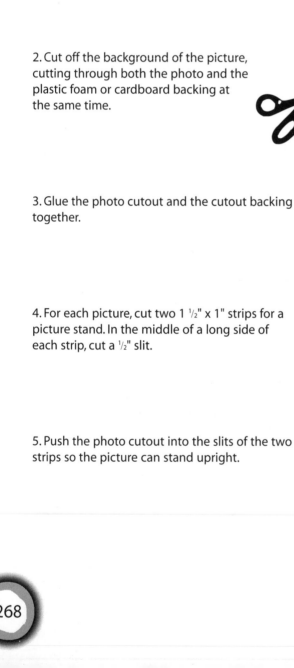

# Recipes

## Out of the Slimy Pit (page 64)
**Slime**

Borax mixture in pitcher:
2 cups water
2 tablespoons borax (from detergent aisle of store)

Glue mixture in bowl:
1/2 cup water
4 drops green food coloring
1/2 cup white school glue

Mix 2 cups water with borax in a pitcher. Stir and set aside. In a large bowl, mix 1/2 cup water, food coloring, and glue. Stir with a plastic spatula. Pour the borax mixture into the bowl and stir rapidly until a glob of slime forms. Drain off the excess liquid. Promptly wash the utensils and dishes. Keep slime away from carpet. The slime can be stored in a sealable plastic bag if the inside of the bag has been coated with cooking spray.

## Hold My Hand (page 92) and Kindness Has Benefits (page 170)
**Cake Mix Cookies**

1 box of cake mix (see below for variations)
1/2 cup salad oil
2 eggs

Preheat oven to 350 degrees. Mix all the ingredients. For round cookies, shape teaspoonfuls of dough into balls. For handprint cookies, roll the dough flat, trace around each family member's hand, and cut out the hands with a blunt knife. Place the balls or hand shapes on an ungreased, foil-lined cookie sheet. Bake for approximately 10 minutes, until golden brown.

Fun variations:
Chocolate chip cookies—yellow or white cake mix with 6 ounces chocolate chips and 1/2 cup chopped pecans
Chocolate-covered cherry cookies—cherry cake mix with chocolate chips
Carrot cookies—carrot cake mix with 1/2 cup raisins and 1/2 cup chopped pecans
Butter pecan cookies—butter cake mix with 1/2 cup chopped pecans
Spice cookies—spice cake mix

# Helping Your Child
## Trust Jesus

Explain the following truths to your child. If he understands and believes them, he is probably ready to put his trust in Jesus as his personal Savior and Lord. If so, pray with him. Then call your local church to discuss how your church welcomes children into the family of God. Rejoice! That's what's happening in heaven (Luke 15:10).

### 1. God loves us and wants us to live forever with him.
*"For God so loved the world that he gave his one and only Son, that whoever believes in him shall not perish but have eternal life" (John 3:16).*

### 2. We have sinned.
*Anyone, then, who knows the good he ought to do and doesn't do it, sins (James 4:17).*

*If we claim to be without sin, we deceive ourselves and the truth is not in us (1 John 1:8).*

### 3. Because of our sins, we do not deserve to live forever with God.
*For all have sinned and fall short of the glory of God (Romans 3:23).*

*For the wages of sin is death, but the gift of God is eternal life in Christ Jesus our Lord (Romans 6:23).*

### 4. Jesus died on the cross to take the punishment we deserve. He is the only way to heaven. We can't get there by trying to be good.
*He was delivered over to death for our sins and was raised to life for our justification (Romans 4:25).*

*Jesus answered, "I am the way and the truth and the life. No one comes to the Father expect through me" (John 14:6).*

*Know that a man is not justified by observing the law, but by faith in Jesus Christ (Galatians 2:16).*

**5. We need to repent (turn away from sin) and trust Jesus as Savior (the one who saves) and Lord (the one who rules over us).**

*"I have declared to both Jews and Greeks that they must turn to God in repentance and have faith in our Lord Jesus" (Acts 20:21).*

*"Salvation is found in no one else, for there is no other name under heaven given to men by which we must be saved" (Acts 4:12).*

*That if you confess with your mouth, "Jesus is Lord," and believe in your heart that God raised him from the dead, you will be saved (Romans 10:9).*

*Peter replied, "Repent and be baptized, every one of you, in the name of Jesus Christ for the forgiveness of your sins. And you will receive the gift of the Holy Spirit" (Acts 2:38).*

**6. If Jesus is our Lord, it will show by how loving we are to others.**

*This is how we know who the children of God are and who the children of the devil are: Anyone who does not do what is right is not a child of God; nor is anyone who does not love his brother (1 John 3:10).*

*Whoever does not love does not know God, because God is love (1 John 4:8).*

*"By this all men will know that you are my disciples, if you love one another" (John 13:35).*

## Books by Tracy Harrast

*Not-So-Quiet Times: 240 Family Devotions Based on the Words of Jesus*
*Not-So-Quiet Times 2: 240 Family Devotions From Psalms and Proverbs*
*Picture That! Bible Storybook*
*My Mommy & Me Story Bible*
*One to Grow On Series: My Bible ABCs*
*One to Grow On Series: My Bible Animals*
*One to Grow On Series: My Bible Colors*
*One to Grow On Series: My Bible Numbers*
*Peek-a-Bible: The Lost and Found Lamb*
*Peek-a-Bible: The Big Boat Ride*
*Peek-a-Bible: The Christmas Story*
*Peek-a-Bible: Little David and Big Goliath*
*Peek-a-Bible: Jonah Goes Overboard*
*Peek-a-Bible: The Easter Story* (available soon)
*Peek-a-Bible: Joseph and the Big Dreams*
*Bible Lessons for Young Readers* (with several authors)
*Bible Puzzle Time: God's People Become a Nation*
*The Life and Lessons of Jesus: Jesus Is Born!*
*The Life and Lessons of Jesus: Jesus Grows Up*
*The Life and Lessons of Jesus: Jesus Prepares to Serve*
*The Life and Lessons of Jesus: Following Jesus*
*The Life and Lessons of Jesus: Names of Jesus*
*The Life and Lessons of Jesus: Learning to Love Like Jesus*
*The Life and Lessons of Jesus: Jesus Shows God's Love*
*The Life and Lessons of Jesus: Jesus Heals*
*The Life and Lessons of Jesus: Jesus Works Miracles*
*The Life and Lessons of Jesus: Jesus Teaches Me to Pray*
*The Life and Lessons of Jesus: Jesus' Last Week*
*The Life and Lessons of Jesus: Jesus Is Alive!*